3/99

D1067953

DISCARD

Andres Duany and Elizabeth Plater-Zyberk

TOWNS AND TOWN-MAKING PRINCIPLES

Andres Duany and Elizabeth Plater-Zyberk

TOWNS AND TOWN-MAKING PRINCIPLES

Edited by
Alex Krieger
with
William Lennertz

Essays by
Alex Krieger ,,, [et al]
Leon Krier
William Lennertz
Patrick Pinnell
Vincent Scully, Jr.

Harvard University Graduate School of Design

RIZZOLI
NEW YORK

Andres Duany and Elizabeth Plater-Zyberk: Towns and Town-Making Principles is one of a series of publications of Harvard University Graduate School of Design, 48 Quincy Street, Cambridge, Massachusetts 02138. This catalogue was published in connection with an exhibition of work by Andres Duany and Elizabeth Plater-Zyberk, Visiting Design Critics in Urban Planning and Design, in the fall of 1990 at the Gund Hall Gallery.

Library of Congress Catalog Card Number   91-71811
International Standard Book Number   0-8478-1436-X

Trade edition published in the United States of America in 1991 by Rizzoli International Publications, Inc. 300 Park Avenue South, New York, NY 10010

Design: Allen + Chin, Boston, Massachusetts

The text of this catalogue was set in Janson by Monotype Composition, Boston, Massachusetts and was printed on Monadnock Dulcet by Meridian Printing, East Greenwich, Rhode Island.

Cover: The master plan of Seaside, Florida.

CONTENTS

The Harvard University Graduate School of Design gratefully acknowledges the generous contributions of the following in support of this publication:

Joseph Alfandre & Company, Inc.
Alfandre, Plater-Zyberk, and Duany Research Corporation

Mr. Gerald W. Blakeley, Jr.
Blakeley Investment Company

Mr. Arnold B. Chace, Jr.
Fields Point Limited Partnership

John A. Clark Company
Haymount Limited Partnership
W.C. & A.N. Miller Development Company

Mr. Peter Kanavos, Jr.
Flag Development Company, Inc.

Mr. and Mrs. Galen Weston
Mr. and Mrs. Geoffrey Kent
Windsor

Corepoint Corporation
Wellington

Foreword

The period shortly after 1950 marked something of a watershed in American life as the majority of Americans became suburbanites for the first time in history. Statistically speaking, between 1950 and 1955, the proportion of suburban development in the United States pushed past fifty percent, continuing to rise to about sixty-five percent by the last census count in 1980. A refurbished housing industry, finally backed by federal government loan guarantees, had quickly recovered by 1949 to prewar and predepression production levels of one million units annually, of which almost eighty percent were in the form of single-family detached houses.

Transportation, especially high-speed interregional highways, opened up the countryside for metropolitan development, continuing the earlier dispersal of urban functions, but now with significant reconcentrations away from older city centers. The result of this growth and development has been a wholesale transformation of American metropolitan life, in which traditional concepts of community, civic place, and neighborhood have been either overrun or severely threatened.

In spite of these radical changes, however, little serious attention has been paid to the contemporary suburban-metropolitan phenomenon within either the design professions or the academic setting of design schools. Consequently, as we approach the end of the century in which suburban and ex-urban life became an essential experience for most Americans, designers have little new to offer and, sadly, a greatly diminished role in the collective process of settlement-making.

Fortunately, the work of Andres Duany and Elizabeth Plater-Zyberk is a conspicuous exception to this pattern of neglect and has almost single-handedly served to recenter discussion of American urbanism towards a broader consideration of metropolitan development. What follows in this volume is the first compilation of their town planning efforts, including documentation of their unusual, on-site "charrette" process.

Alex Krieger places Duany and Plater-Zyberk's work into an insightful urban design perspective while William Lennertz provides a useful insider's view. Vincent Scully's essay is a most welcome addition for, as both a mentor and a proponent of their work, he has exerted a considerable influence. Patrick Pinnell offers the perspective of a sometime collaborator. The afterword by Leon Krier focuses on probably Duany and Plater-Zyberk's most lasting contribution — the codes by which their town planning principles are realized and put into action. Finally, Duany and Plater-Zyberk's strong commitments to innovative teaching and practice are both well known. For our part, we at the Graduate School of Design are pleased to help give this important work on town design well-deserved and coherent recognition.

Peter G. Rowe
Raymond Garbe Professor of
Architecture and Urban Design
Chairman, Department of
Urban Planning and Design
Harvard University
Graduate School of Design

Alex Krieger

Since (and Before)
Seaside

A decade ago Andres Duany and Elizabeth Plater-Zyberk, along with their patron Robert Davis, began to create the town of Seaside, a modestly scaled resort community rather remotely located in the Florida panhandle. Eventually to include some 350 houses on eighty acres, Seaside has emerged as the most celebrated new American community. The breadth of its fame is astonishing. It has been acclaimed in the halls of academe, at national conventions of home builders, by the Prince of Wales, and in *Newsweek, The Smithsonian,* and even *Travel and Leisure.*

Seaside is a remarkable place worthy of acclaim *(Fig. 1)*. Indeed, it has been the catalyst for the exploration of alternatives to conventional suburban land planning which is the subject of this monograph. The extent of its acclaim, however, also reminds us how miserably bereft of character most of our communities, particularly post-World War II suburban ones, seem by comparison.

Our predicament is this: we admire one kind of place—Marblehead, Massachusetts, for example—but we consistently build something very different, the more familiar sprawl of modern suburbia *(Figs. 2, 3)*. Our planning tools—notably our zoning ordinances—facilitate segmented, decentralized suburban growth while actually making it impossible to incorporate qualities that we associate with towns such as Marblehead. Few ordinances tolerate (much less encourage) the concentration of uses, the multiplicity of scales, the redundancy of streets, and the hierarchical fabric of public spaces which characterize the towns of our memory and our travels.

We also live in an age of broad public concern for the physical environment. Yet we are preoccupied at the periphery of what is essential about town-making. On the one hand, planners seem mired in the bureaucratic realm of policy formulation and resource management—important, certainly, though not often enough seen as related to the spatial dimension of communities. On the other hand, architects (and for that matter citizens who make up planning and design review boards) are consumed with detail and image: aesthetic guidelines, for example, or worse, motifs for simulating various architectural periods. Consequently, we continue to build—and live in—vast tracts of undifferentiated development that form neither neighborhoods, towns, or cities.

There is no shortage of criticism levelled at such modern development. Alternatives, however, are in short supply—especially ones which retain the qualities that have made such development desirable and economically advantageous for so many. Towards this end Duany and Plater-Zyberk have pursued a threefold mission. 1) They advocate designing suburban subdivisions

2

3

1

in the manner of towns. 2) They challenge zoning conventions and write codes that favor traditional patterns of placemaking. 3) They work directly with those who produce the modern suburban landscape, the real estate developers, with the aim of persuading them of alternatives.[1]

When Conventional Wisdom Fails. Behaving like ostriches, many architects, and town planners prefer to ignore the suburb, hoping somehow that the suburb will prove as inconsequential as it is distasteful. Most of us, after all, see ourselves as urbanists: lovers of cities where culture and civic space interact naturally. And because we believe this, we assume that the city and city values are ubiquitous while the suburbs are some aberrant form of settlement.

Andres Duany and Elizabeth Plater-Zyberk have lifted their heads to survey the cul-de-sac, and have discovered what is so hard for us to admit: that the suburb, not the city, is ubiquitous in modern American life. And they reason that unless we confront the suburb directly — by understanding both its hold on the American imagination and its liabilities — the liabilities will overwhelm us!

They are right. Ignoring the new "cityscapes" of Las Colinas, Texas, or Tyson's Corner, Virginia, or of the Houston outside its perimeter beltway, while placing great faith in the occasional evidence of gentrification within the older sections of mostly eastern seaboard cities, is unlikely to bring the planning professions any great new insights about contemporary urbanism.[2] As a civilization we are still spreading outward at an alarming rate, voraciously consuming land and resources, and stretching to disfigurement the bonds which have bound us in communities.

4

Such spreading outward is natural to Americans, *(Fig. 4)* but often results from planning initiatives designed to control it. The last tide of planned decentralization in this country occurred under the aegis of the 1960s Federal New Town Program. New communities such as Columbia, Maryland and Reston, Virginia were posited as alternatives, on the one hand, to overgrown older cities, and on the other, to unplanned suburban sprawl.[3] While Columbia and Reston were conceived as a means of "urbanizing" suburban patterns, many consider their influence to be the opposite — of serving as a model for suburbanizing the centers of cities in order for cities to be able to compete with the perceived advantages of places like Columbia. Poignantly, the American New Town Program was among the many stray roots of the British Garden City Movement, both a point of origin, and a nemesis for Duany and Plater-Zyberk's work.[4]

Although labelled neotraditionalists because they invoke ancient planning principles and depict classic images of town design, Duany and Plater-Zyberk have actually been peering into the future at this dominant decentralization and, one could say, domineering form of settlement. Their mission is to alert us to the consequences of pursuing this future by emphasizing the cost at which conveniences such as easy mobility and a preference for privacy over sociability have been purchased.

In focusing on the suburbs, however, they are aware that there are no quick remedies, including Seaside, or singular scapegoats (as convenient as they may seem) such as the automobile.

5

The foundations for the suburb are far too deeply embedded in American life, with weaknesses and strengths that are not always easily separated.

Suburban Aspirations.   The contemporary American suburban landscape is a victim of its own success. We were seeking its advantages long before the automobile materialized to make them conveniently accessible *(Fig. 5)*. Hardly an aberrant form of settlement, the leafy suburb between city and country is precisely the form of settlement that the western world has desired since the Enlightenment. Carl Marx's villain, the "idiocy of rural life," and the Rousseauian "artificialities of over-civilization" were both to be overcome by constructing a radical new landscape between the geographies associated with each domain.[5]

What had for a millenium been a binary world of city *or* country would now make way for what Ebenezer Howard called the "third magnet," city *and* country. A pre-eighteenth century mind could hardly have conceived that the forlorn and marginally inhabited zone directly outside of the city walls, which for centuries denoted "a place of inferior, debased and especially licentious habits of life," would now expand to encompass a territory in which all would reside.[6] By the end of the nineteenth century the transformation of the loathsome *suburbe* would be complete as it became the safe haven from the monstrous and even more loathsome industrial city, dubbed by a contemporary of Charles Dickens "The City of Dreadful Night."[7]

During its first century-and-a-half, the advantages of this new territory between city and country reigned: fresh air, greenery, and space; solitude without loss of proximity to society; a place for nurturing family and for cultivating one's homestead; a refuge from industry, competitiveness, and social stress. Coral Gables, where Duany and Plater-Zyberk live, is such a middle landscape, and neither they nor we can easily be displaced from such environments.

The risks associated with the construction of this middle landscape have emerged more slowly, becoming manifest only as more of us have achieved access to it. The risk is diabolically simple: once we all occupy the middle we have destroyed the extremes relative to which the advantages of the middle might be measured. Without city or country can the suburb have any meaning?

This is not a rhetorician's dilemma. Most contemporary environments cannot be historically understood as either urban or rural, though they appear to offer many of the choices and opportunities associated with town life – all, that is, except for propinquity, probably the most important criterion for true civility. In an age of instant communication and mobility it is easy, but wrongheaded, to assume that physical proximity is no longer essential for urbanity *(Fig. 6)*.

So while Americans keep dreaming of a good place to live, many of our dreams – to live in the presence of nature; to live near city and country; to own and control our own property; to have constant freedom of movement; to move up; to move away; to start again; to portray our individuality; to cherish our privacy – all tend to work against establishing good communities in which to live.

6

7

8

9

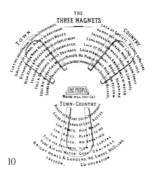

10

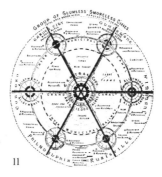

11

The Town: Here, Not Everywhere. In arguing for his not-so-imaginary Broadacres, Frank Lloyd Wright demanded that it be "everywhere or nowhere."[8] He was dreaming of an omnipresent if technologically sophisticated countryside. We have instead achieved an omnipresent suburbia. To break through its homogeneities a familiar antidote, the town, presents itself just as it did a century ago when the task was to find alternatives to the demoralizing Victorian city.

Duany and Plater-Zyberk are at the forefront of a group of planners and architects who have begun to argue that, since many suburban subdivisions are conceived at a scale that exceeds the size of historic towns, we should turn to the principles that have always governed town design to design new suburbs.[9] In so doing, they assert, we might harness runaway development in the service of more sociable, manageable, and urbane living—town life instead of housesitting, street-strolling instead of strip-cruising, front porches in addition to backyards.

This is not a new but a remembered idea. The early planned suburbs inevitably aspired to be towns, albeit pastoral ones, in which to escape from the neighboring urban colossus. This remembered ideal brings together a diverse legion of committed (if often frustrated) town planners across a century and across oceans: Clarence Stein, Henry Wright, Lewis Mumford, Clarence Perry, and John Nolen in the United States; Joseph von Steuben, Theodor Fritsch, Georg Metzendorf, Ernst May and Leberecht Migge in Germany; Georges Benoit-Levy, Henri Sellier and Tony Garnier in France; Stanley Abercrombie, Patrick Geddes, Frederic Osborn, Barry Parker, Raymond Unwin, and finally, unavoidably, Ebenezer Howard in England.[10] It is not a list of kindred spirits. Many on it would be aghast at the inclusion of several of the others, as no doubt would Duany and Plater-Zyberk, who acknowledge other sources such as Leon Krier, Werner Hegemann, Albert Peets, and Camillo Sitte for their work.[11] There is, however, a binding agent. It is the belief in the scale and spatial organization of the traditional town as the basic building block for human settlement *(Figs. 7, 8, 9)*.

The clearest codification of this at the scale of a modern region was Ebenezer Howard's Garden City which, ironically, has more often been blamed for unleashing the forces of modern suburbia.[12] While anticipating the attraction of the third magnet—the city-country—for modern society, he imagined it to be composed (like a complex biological cell) of many discrete settlements occupying a regional garden, and kept apart by the countervailing force of legislation *(Figs. 10, 11)*. His ambition was to dissect the swollen industrial city into many self-sufficient, spatially identifiable, railroad-linked, finite, communally-owned, cooperatively-administered towns. There is no more compelling vision of a universe of towns in the annals of planning theory. Unfortunately, instead of self-sufficient towns, it begat the parasitic *garden suburb*, which many of Howard's disciples unwittingly produced.

In a handful of instances Howard's ideal was physically approximated: in the pre-Howard garden village of New Earswick *(Fig. 12)* by Parker and Unwin; in the even earlier industrial villages of Port Sunlight and Bournville, whose influence Howard acknowledged; and in the post-Letch-

12

13

14

15

16

worth garden village of Margarethenhöhe for the Krupp family in Essen, a virtual ode to Raymond Unwin's treatise on town planning.[13] Alas, the majority of attempts following Letchworth *(Fig. 13)* and Hampstead, the first planned garden cities, stopped short of this standard except occasionally in appearance and even less frequently in layout. Parker and Unwin, Howard's planning and architectural facilitators, must bear some of the responsibility *(Fig. 14)*. As Peter Hall has written of Letchworth, "Unwin-Parker architecture clothed the Howard skeleton so memorably that, ever after, people could hardly distinguish one from the other."[14] Subsequent to Unwin-Parker, the architecture—as clothing—frequently superseded the emphasis on organizational principles which they themselves held to be of first priority.

When beautifully executed at the hands of a Raymond Unwin, or via the collaboration of the Olmsted brothers and Grosvenor Atterbury at Forest Hills Gardens in Queens *(Fig. 15)*, the garden suburb *appears* to satisfy Howard's vision, though not its politics, social organization, or economic self-sufficiency. As reproduced indiscriminately throughout the western world for the past century the garden suburb ceased even to attempt to simulate the physical organization of a town, much less to host its social and political structures.

Here lies one of the major weaknesses of Howard's legacy and one of the most formidable challenges for Duany and Plater-Zyberk. It is easier to sketch or even build a town fragment than it is to achieve an actual town. How does one recover the physical planning principles that seem to make good towns without succumbing to mere appearances and producing simulacrum towns? The risk of debasement is great. In an environment of mass-market consumption where fads run amok, can one keep any subdivision with picket fences and a gazebo from being trumpeted as a traditional town? Duany and Plater-Zyberk's method is to work directly with the makers of the suburb. Using marketing devices familiar to the real estate developer, Duany and Plater-Zyberk lure them with potent imagery into the realm of planning principles.

Pragmatic Idealism. Substituting appearances for reality is common among those who develop real estate at a large scale. Knowing this, Duany and Plater-Zyberk chart a perilous course between principle and caricature, relying on representation to entice their clients to commit to the principles. A high percentage of their clients do so, with the fervor of neophytes, becoming themselves advocates for town-making.

Duany and Plater-Zyberk's typical presentation for a town plan incorporates both highly specific technical codes and a series of perspective vignettes which purport to show the plan's town-like qualities. Many of the vignettes would make fine greeting cards *(Fig. 16)*. They are shockingly sentimental, but play an important didactic role. They trigger a collective appreciation of precisely the ambiance that most contemporary environments lack, but which any good developer hopes (and often promises) will characterize his project. The sketches are presented to the developer as the rational consequence of following a set of simple, codifiable, rules of land planning without which the scenes could not be realized. Critics who question the overt sentimentalism overlook the more pragmatic intent of these renderings. They are Duany and Plater-Zyberk's own marketing tool for validating the principles which they seek to disseminate.

The vignettes serve another didactic purpose. Cognizant of their clients' tendency to use traditional imagery in selling model subdivisions, Duany and Plater-Zyberk use the vignettes to distinguish between the typically vulgar renditions of historic styles, and more refined depictions of classical or vernacular-inspired idioms. Here too, Duany and Plater-Zyberk are teaching their clients — about the historic prototypes and architectural traditions upon which they sometimes carelessly rely, and to exhibit more discriminating aesthetic judgment.

Duany and Plater-Zyberk operate best in the trenches, admonishing, cajoling, occasionally shaming those most responsible for producing the suburban landscape: the private land developer, the zoning official and (increasingly) the traffic engineer. In the tradition of Daniel Burnham's legendary capacity to convince his clients that good design is good business, Duany and Plater-Zyberk relentlessly sell the practicality of the town ideal. Such salesmanship earns them much respect from their developer clients who sense that this pair are not naive theoreticians, but pragmatists with a vision.

Beyond Seaside. The four-day work week, long anticipated by optimistic efficiency experts and leisure-seekers, may shortly be upon us, but for unanticipated reasons. In Los Angeles, the premier middle landscape of a generation ago *(Fig. 17)*, the recently established South Coast Air Quality Management District has proposed radical legislation to mitigate air pollution and traffic congestion. Among the compulsory restrictions will be altering the work day and work week in an effort to reduce commuter traffic congestion and resultant pollution. But the real villain in the Los Angeles basin is the settlement pattern, not the work day. Without radical land use legislation to alter it the South Coast Air Quality Management District will ultimately fail in its mission.

This, then, is the next challenge for Duany and Plater-Zyberk as they begin their second decade of work. To respond to it they must paradoxically alter their arena of operations. They have been operating at the edge of the expanding city, persuading those with a few hundred acres of as yet undeveloped land to develop it more thoughtfully, more environmentally soundly, more urbanely. This was the logical first point of intervention. Out there at the edge of urbanization, the absence of constraints and the availability of land most often produces the most banal and least town-like patterns of settlement.

However, even when inspired by notions of traditional patterns of settlement, such continual expansion, so uniquely American, harms all existing towns. It obviates the need to settle in and improve what exists, to reuse, to revitalize, to retain critical urban densities. It perpetuates the belief that in starting over again we can do it better this time. But it is precisely the perpetual new start that accelerates the building of needless infrastructure, impinges further upon virgin land and ecological systems, enables additional social and economic segregation, and devalues the places left behind.

17

In truth we have been moving to places like Los Angeles from traditional towns, which have served as settings for a cyclical drama involving first abandonment and then idealization. For each wave of renewed interest in town life, there have been equal waves of escape, first to the big city but increasingly during this century to the suburbs-near-the-city. For each Mumfordian sentiment about the organicism of small town life, there has been a Sinclair Lewis proclaiming that life to be "tediousness made tangible . . . dullness made God."[15]

Despite recurring desires, we cannot literally return to the New England village: its homes and institutions surrounding the common and itself surrounded by productive and pastoral fields. That does not mean that we shouldn't attempt to make new suburban development more town-like. But, more importantly, we should cherish the towns that we have made, while tempering our anticipation for the success of the next new traditional town. In seeking to recapture the advantages of the town, Duany and Plater-Zyberk have made us aware of how much has been lost. Now we must learn to value, to maintain, and to refine those thousands of towns—not to mention suburbs in search of "townness"—already built but languishing *(Fig. 18)*. A commitment to the revival of these must be understood to be as essential—and urbane—a goal as to build anew.

Civilizing the Suburb. The Latin roots for the medieval English *suburbium* refer to a place *beyond* or outside of the city.[16] The Greek word for suburb, *proasteion,* originally referred to something *before* the city. This etymological distinction is crucial for the task ahead. Common wisdom still assumes the suburb to be separate from the city. Like the ancient Greeks, Duany and Plater-Zyberk prefer to think of the modern suburb as a rudimentary form of habitation, something which precedes the city and thus in need of civilizing. This catalogue—the first though surely not the last compilation of the town planning projects of Andres Duany and Elizabeth Plater-Zyberk—suggests how the effort to civilize the suburb might commence.

18

Alex Krieger is Adjunct Professor of Architecture and Urban Design, and Director of the Urban Planning and Design Programs at Harvard University Graduate School of Design.

Illustrations

1
Seaside, Florida as it exists in 1990.

2
Marblehead, Massachusetts.

3
Plan of the Golden Triangle *in Framingham, Massachusetts, a typical commercial strip consuming several times the land area of a traditional downtown. Characteristically, nearly half of the land is devoted to parking.*

4
An apparently limitless landscape fostered nineteenth-century expansion. Characteristic bird's eye view: Prescott, Arizona, circa 1879.

5
Elm Avenue, Hartford, Connecticut.

6
View of Mashpee Commons, Mashpee, Massachusetts, a new downtown taking shape directly over a strip shopping center. Like a nineteenth-century frontier town, it is showing great promise.

7
Plan of Hampstead Garden Suburb, Parker and Unwin, 1937.

8
Plan of the garden village of Margarethenhöhe, Essen, 1912.

9
Plan of Mariemont, near Cincinnati, John Nolen, 1921.

10

The Three Magnets as illustrated in Howard's Garden Cities of Tomorrow.

11

Howard's diagram of a constellation of garden cities.

12

A typical residential street in New Earswick, York, circa 1913.

13

Aerial view of the town center in 1937, Letchworth Garden City.

14

A characteristic Parker and Unwin sketch, in this instance of Hampstead Garden Suburb.

15

Contemporary view of the town center at Forest Hills Gardens, Queens, 1912. Note the influence of Parker and Unwin's architecture.

16

Sketch of Haymount, Duany and Plater-Zyberk, 1989.

17

Idyllic view of Los Angeles as we would like to believe it still exists.

18

Brockton, Massachusetts. A traditional town languishing in decay and neglect.

Notes

1 Duany and Plater-Zyberk's efforts to produce alternate forms of zoning are the specific subject of the final chapter of this monograph on pages 95–103.

2 Awareness of such new "cityscapes" is increasing. See, for example, "The New Boom Towns" in *The Wall Street Journal*, March 27, 1989, p.B1; "Brave New World" in *Landscape Architecture*, December, 1988, a special issue devoted to what they call "edge cities;" and Robert Fishman, "Beyond Suburbia: The Rise of the Technoburb," *Bourgeois Utopias: The Rise and Fall of Suburbia* (New York 1987), pp. 182–207. See also an early anticipation of this new type of city in Jean Gottmann, *Megalopolis* (Cambridge, Massachusetts, 1961).

3 Reston today is in the midst of a major effort to urbanize its center. See Philip Langdon, "Pumping Up Suburban Downtowns," *Planning*, July 1990, pp. 22–28.

4 For the philosophical roots of the American new town movement see Clarence S. Stein, *Toward New Towns for America*. Refer to the edition with Lewis Mumford's introduction (Cambridge, Massachusetts, 1973).

5 A large literature has developed around this theme of a "middle landscape." See in particular: Leo Marx, *The Machine in the Garden: Technology and the Pastoral Ideal in America* (New York, 1964); James L. Machor, *Pastoral Cities: Urban Ideals and the Symbolic Landscape of America* (Madison, Wisconsin, 1987); and David Schuyler, *The New Urban Landscape: The Redefinitions of City Form in Nineteenth-Century America* (Baltimore, 1986).

6 Quoted from the *Oxford English Dictionary* in Fishman, op. cit., p.6.

7 J. Thomson, *The City of Dreadful Night and Other Poems* (London, 1880).

8 Between 1932 and 1958, in five separate book-length publications and numerous articles, Frank Lloyd Wright extolled the virtues of his own version of the third magnet. See the special edition of *Architectural Record* devoted to the initial Broadacres plan (April 1935).

9 Among other current advocates for designing the suburbs using small town analogies see: Peter Calthorpe, et al., *The Pedestrian Pocket Book: A New Suburban Design Strategy* (University of Washington, 1988).

10 For a good general overview of the international scope of the garden city movement see: Simon Pepper, guest editor, "The Garden City Idea," *Architectural Review*, June 1978, pp. 321–376.

11 Duany and Plater-Zyberk often credit Leon Krier for inspiring their work. They, in turn, were responsible for his involvement in Seaside where he designed a house for himself, his first built work in America. Currently they are collaborating on a new town in England—Poundbury—for the Prince of Wales. It is designed by Krier, and coded (zoned) by Duany and Plater-Zyberk. Among their most well-thumbed reference works are Werner Hegemann and Elbert Peets, *The American Vitruvius: An Architect's Handbook of Civic Art*, initially published in 1922 and reissued (with a preface by Leon Krier) in 1988 by the Princeton Architectural Press.

12 Ebenezer Howard's book was first published in 1898 as *Tomorrow: a Peaceful Path to Real Reform*, and reissued with slight revisions as *Garden Cities of Tomorrow* in 1902. It was this later edition that won him international fame and coined a new concept of city.

13 Raymond Unwin, *Town Planning in Practice: An Introduction to the Art of Designing Cities and Suburbs* (London, 1909). In the Sitte tradition (though Unwin claimed that he only became familiar with Sitte's work afterwards), this quickly became one of the foundation texts for the then emerging new discipline of planning. Among such turn-of-the-century treatises on town planning it was unique in including suburbs in its title. Andres Duany claims that even today more insight on town planning can be found in this book than in the typical urban planning school curriculum.

14 Peter Hall, *Cities of Tomorrow: An Intellectual History of Urban Planning and Design in the Twentieth Century* (Oxford, 1988). Paperback edition, 1990, p. 97.

15 Sinclair Lewis, *Main Street* (New York, 1920), p. 257. There is a wealth of American literature inspired by the small town, and equally divided, seemingly, between projecting a sentimental or a condescending view of small town life. If Lewis's Gopher Prairie, Minnesota furnishes a stiff dose of the condescending view, then Thornton Wilder's 1938 play, *Our Town*, modelled upon Peterborough, New Hampshire, epitomizes the sentimental view. A good account of America's complex relationship to its small towns is found in Richard Lingeman, *Small Town America: A Narrative, 1620–the Present* (Boston, 1980).

16 For illuminating discussions about the origins and varying meanings of the term suburb see the opening chapters in Robert Fishman, op. cit. Kenneth T. Jackson, *Crabgrass Frontier: The Suburbanization of the United States* (New York, 1985); and John R. Stilgoe, *Borderland: Origins of the American Suburb, 1820–1939* (New Haven, 1988).

Vincent Scully, Jr.

Seaside and New Haven

The work of Andres Duany and Elizabeth Plater-Zyberk represents a major advance in the massive revival of the vernacular and classical traditions of architecture which has taken place during the past thirty years. One is tempted to say that it represents the most important step in that historical development, because it is the one which deals with architecture in its true dimension, that of the city as a whole. So in the movement begun in architectural practice and theory at least, advanced by Robert Venturi and Charles Moore, and carried along in their own ways by Aldo Rossi, Leon Krier, and Robert Stern, Duany and Plater-Zyberk have moved in to occupy the key position. It is they who have most convincingly worked out the way to fit buildings inspired by tradition into traditional urban groupings, so creating a decent environment for human habitation once again.

In an urban and suburban world whose amenities for living had been measurably diminished by both the iconoclastic theories of Modernism and the dull bureaucrats who write the planning codes, Duany and Plater-Zyberk learned how to reverse the destructive theory by rewriting the idiot codes. This was certainly the key. Duany and Plater-Zyberk perceived that the codes were the answer, that the solution lay in conceptualizing the problems of streets and buildings alike and of dictating their forms through the medium of language.

That perception itself represented powers of observation and conceptualization of a very high order, and here Duany and Plater-Zyberk showed themselves to be enormously gifted at the very beginning of their careers. When they entered Yale's graduate program in architecture in 1971, they came into an intellectual environment where, in history at least, the vernacular and classical traditions of architecture were sympathetically studied and treated as an integral part of the development of modern architecture as a whole, while the destructive effects of International Style urbanism, as cataclysmically evident in urban redevelopment, had been recognized and condemned in print. However, that phrase, "the development of modern architecture," still had a conceptual blindness built into it. Modernism retained a special aura. The past, however integral to the evolution of Modernism or however preferable to it, was in fact, past.

I had been writing about the Stick and Shingle styles since 1947, but still felt the existence of some strangely impassable barrier between the nineteenth-century past and the late twentieth-century present. It would never have occurred to me that the turned posts of the Stick Style could be used once again exactly as they had once been used, or that the screened porch, the most genial architectural environment ever created in the United States, could be directly revived. And though I had deplored the destruction of the traditional street and recognized the beautiful urban structure of house, lot, sidewalk, grass strip, curb, and vehicular way that had shaped most American towns, it did not seem to me that architects would ever again be able to shape that intricate urban structure. We were blinded by the horrid Germanic concept of the *zeitgeist*, whereby "our time," through some peculiarly and probably magical mechanism of its own, absolutely forbade us to do certain things —and in architecture and urbanism almost everything worth doing.

We ask ourselves now how we could have been so blinded. Clearly enough, there were some formidable social and intellectual forces at work upon us that drove us mad. I think, personally, that it was World War I that did it. It quite naturally drove the Europeans crazy, so that, despite innumerable utopian visions before the war, it was only afterward that LeCorbusier on the one hand, and Hilberseimer on the other, could dream of the total obliteration of the traditional city. In LeCorbusier's version a few monuments of the past remained standing; in Hilberseimer's, none. Strange, too, that the new social force, the automobile, became the favored engine of destruction in both cases. After World War II, the automobile came into its own, most of all in the United States, where the automobile industry managed to get our trolley lines torn up and where we embarked on the joyride that left our cities in ruins. The automobile triumphed over us. We designed everything for it, "to keep it happy," as Duany says.

That destruction of traditional urbanism was fine for the late modernists: they wanted to strut their stuff in chaos anyway. The rest of us knew that it was a tragedy based on uncivilized promises and clearly serving an evil rather than a desirable social end. Among other things, it savagely destroyed many fine low-income neighborhoods no less than the fabric of Downtown. Yet, even though Venturi had already written that "Main Street [was] almost all right," most of us still labored in large part under the modernist spell, the jealous conceptions of a hermetic style.

But not Duany and Plater-Zyberk. From the first days that I knew them, they saw. Why they were so favored I do not really know, but they were uniquely able, as only the most free of human beings are able, to cut through preconception and to see what is. First they saw detail. They led me and the rest of our class through the streets of New Haven, my own city. They showed us the Stick and Shingle houses of Newport and Bar Harbor as they existed right under our noses in their everyday vernacular guise — not only as I had written about them, as objects of historical interest and the precursors of Modernism, but also as direct models for contemporary use.

So we saw the posts and the porches anew, the wood stripping and the shingled surfaces, the frontal gables and, more than that, the front steps, the sidewalks, the grass verge with its trees— once, God help us, great elms. We saw the houses side by side, the lots narrow, the houses tall enough to shape the streets, framed and overarched by the trees. Through the details we thus saw the type, the necessary building type that can shape cities. We came to perceive that Invention, which Modernism, especially late Modernism, had canonized, was wide of the mark and urbanistically very dangerous. It was the type, with its beloved detailing, its decoration, that made urban order and individual variety together. It was, in the great old nineteenth-century aphorism, a matter of decorating construction, not constructing decoration, as Modernism had come to do.

This was architecture, not painting, not abstract art. Duany and Plater-Zyberk saw, most of all, that nothing needed to be abstracted, neither the type nor the detail. They could be used as they were, as Modernism — and through its influence the main paragraphs in the Secretary of the Interior's guidelines for the restoration of old buildings — insisted they (in the name of the *zeitgeist*) could not be. Later, of course, Duany and Plater-Zyberk's own design was stiffened and simplified by the classicism of Leon Krier, but the principle remained the same, and this is their greatest accomplishment: to do it literally. This is the only way it can be done — without being afraid of the fellow who copies LeCorbusier saying, "You're only copying," or, worse, of some triple-dyed moron saying, "It's not intellectual."

So we began to see the city as it had been and might be again. We saw New Haven's Edgewood Avenue with its parkway and its grass strip down the middle, planted in trees, where a few elms still stand. There on that street where I used to run my dog down to Edgewood Park when I was a child, students of mine made me perceive the dignity and sweetness of the kind of two-family house I had lived in as a boy. It was a very great gift, not the only one students have given me, but an important one from which I have profited ever since.

New Haven has profited too. Everywhere throughout the city people are stripping off the vinyl siding and revealing the old skeletal stripping and the shingled gables and rebuilding the porches and screening them, and turning the posts once again; the lumber yards had never really forgotten how to do it. In the neighborhoods and downtown as well, buildings are being preserved which under similar economic circumstances would have been destroyed thirty years ago. The preservation movement itself, which is essential to the life of all human communities, has of course gone hand in hand with the new seeing and the vernacular and classical revivals, and it is, without question, the most powerful popular movement in architecture of the past two hundred years.

But it is essential for the city to have confidence in new building as well and to know how to do it correctly in relation to the old. Here Duany and Plater-Zyberk seem to be on the track for good. It was especially rewarding to see them, after their bout with Arquitectonica, breaking through all at once to their own genius for dealing with the community entire. True enough, it sometimes seemed, in some of the later phases of building at Seaside, for example, that they might be giving way before the pressure of the architectural community to do all the wrong things despite themselves. It is an unfortunate fact that architectural publications and architecture schools as well still put a premium on anticommunal values, on originality, on knocking the viewer's eyes out, on reinventing some square wheel. All too often the decently modest building that gets along with its neighbors to shape an environment doesn't get praised or published, and some primitivistic folly does. That surely happened once or twice at Seaside, despite the entirely appropriate and sometimes inspired work there by Leon Krier, Robert Orr, Melanie Taylor, Deborah Berke, Scott Merrill, and other architects, and not least by the developer himself.

Here it is the place of the code to keep the city civilized, exactly as laws are intended to do. It is not conformity but decent behavior and intelligent conversation that are required, an architecture in the truest sense rationalized. Again, the type and the details. Duany and Plater-Zyberk have, I think, learned that lesson wholly, as all their many later codes decisively show. They know that they cannot avoid dictating forms to a considerable extent, and that, whatever their ingrained bias for freedom, they cannot leave the kind of loophole into which trendy posturing can insert itself to the detriment of the environment as a whole. These have not been palatable lessons for modern architects to learn, nourished as they have been on the romantic ideal of individual glory, but architecture demands that they learn them.

Perhaps Duany and Plater-Zyberk have now done all that architects can do. They have surely done much more than we had come to expect from architects in the twentieth century, and they may well have changed the practice of architecture for generations to come. In order to accomplish all that, however, they have had to work with the realities of the market, however mitigated at first by the patronage of an idealistic developer like Robert Davis, and their new towns have been largely luxury affairs. Although they have increasingly attempted to include what they call "affordable" housing in them, in ways that make urban sense for everybody concerned, they have clearly got to find ways to do more than that in the future.

Here again it is a matter of making people see. In this case it is, I suppose, the federal government which must be made to recognize the end of the Cold War and to reorder its priorities. Proper community living was a major casualty not only of the automobile but also of that economic conflict and, in part, of the brutal late Modernism which was its architectural corollary. Ironically, it was LeCorbusier himself who once posed the issue most clearly: "Des munitions? Non! Des logis, s'il vous plaît!" But it is not a question of "housing" any more; the ghetto must go. The community must revive. Duany and Plater-Zyberk have shown us that this is possible, that it can be done. Hence their developers' communities must be regarded as models of the larger communal revival. If they are not that, they can only be seen in the long run as very beautiful and inexpressibly sad.

Still, one would like to avoid the preachy tone that is all too easy to fall into when urbanistic questions arise. The issue remains, unsentimentally, reality: the beauty of what we have, how to see it as it is and value it for what it is, how to make it, democratically, more complete and the law of the land.

Vincent Scully, Jr. is the Sterling Professor of the History of Art at Yale University.

William Lennertz

Town-Making Fundamentals

The work of Andres Duany and Elizabeth Plater-Zyberk begins with the recognition that design affects behavior. Duany and Plater-Zyberk see the structure and function of a community as interdependent. Because of this, they believe a designer's decisions will permeate the lives of residents not just visually but in the way residents live. They believe design structures functional relationships, quantitatively and qualitatively, and that it is a sophisticated tool whose power exceeds its cosmetic attributes.

Recognizing that healthy communities are complex organic systems, Duany and Plater-Zyberk have developed a methodology of town planning which respects and replicates this inherent complexity. They have gathered a basic set of design principles which they apply through planning charrettes that bring many minds to bear on the multifaceted problem of town design.

Design Principles

Road trips through southern towns with Robert Davis, the developer of Seaside, were the first lessons on town planning for both developer and architects. These towns revealed a pattern of streets, parks, and squares, with houses and their porches close to the street, and strong community bonds. From their observations, Duany and Plater-Zyberk identified the fundamental physical elements that embody community. The black and white diagrams that describe the plan of Seaside exhibit the basic rules in the making of any town. These rules are flexible in accommodating program and place and a natural evolution and growth.

The Master Plan. The master plan is the composite drawing which incorporates all critical information on the town plan *(Fig. 1)*. Its design strategy often follows the pattern typical of American towns: a geometrically defined center radiates an interconnected street network which adapts to existing conditions. The plans for larger communities, created after Seaside, show the ascending hierarchy of neighborhood, village, town, and regional street patterns.

1

The Duany and Plater-Zyberk plan concentrates commercial activity, including shopping and working, in town centers. It distributes civic spaces and buildings throughout the neighborhoods to contribute to their character and focus. Neighborhoods are planned on a quarter-mile radius which results in a five-minute walk from the neighborhood edge to its center.

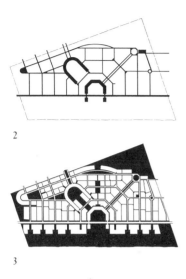

2

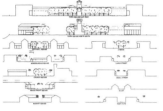

3

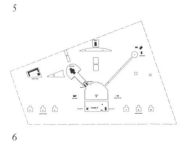

4

5

6

7

Street Network. Streets and squares are the primary public spaces of a town or neighborhood, as well as facilitators of vehicular and pedestrian movement. In those plans created by Duany and Plater-Zyberk, blocks are generally no larger than 230 by 600 feet to ensure that building lots front streets and that traveling distances are reasonable *(Fig. 2)*. New street networks connect whenever possible to existing streets, to become part of a regional network. The layout of streets reflects both the character of the land and the designers' efforts to make a memorable network that will accept future growth in an orderly manner.

Pedestrian Network. Paths through squares and parks, plus mid-block pedestrian alleys, provide the pedestrian routes throughout town, in addition to the street and sidewalk system *(Fig. 3)*.

Street Sections. The street sections drawn for each town or neighborhood depict the character of the streets *(Fig. 4)*. The intention is to make a place where pedestrians feel comfortable as well as to provide for automobile travel. The proportion of adjacent building heights to the street width is specified to establish the character of the street and its spatial role in the overall town plan. The careful detailing of travel and parking lanes (with parallel parking wherever possible to protect the pedestrian), the alignment of trees and other plantings, the sidewalk width, and build-to lines, are all variables in the design of streets that characterize and distinguish neighborhoods.

The Regulating Plan. The zoning of building types reflects the principle of integration, rather than separation, of uses *(Fig. 5)*. Dwellings, shops, and workplaces, are located in close proximity to each other.

Public Buildings and Squares. Squares and parks are distributed throughout the neighborhoods. They are designed as settings for informal social activity and recreation as well as larger civic gatherings. Civic buildings, planned in coordination with public open spaces, are prominently sited, ideally terminating vistas and enclosing streets to serve as landmarks. These buildings serve to house social, cultural, or religious activities *(Fig. 6)*.

The Codes. The codes are a series of documents that ensures the implementation of the town design *(Fig. 7)*. The Urban Regulations control those aspects of private building which pertain to the formation of public spaces. The Architectural Regulations control the materials, configurations, and construction techniques of the buildings. In a town built without the benefit of centuries or a diversity of founders, the codes encourage variety while ensuring the harmony required to give character to a community.

The design principles shown in the diagrams address numerous growth management issues that are commonly considered political concerns: traffic congestion, air pollution, parking, and affordable housing, among others. Traffic congestion and pollution are diminished by the interconnecting network of streets and by the reduction of vehicular trips that pedestrian-oriented design encourages.

On-street parking is permitted wherever possible in order to control traffic speed, protect the pedestrian, and distribute the required parking load. In the town center, small parking lots or structures are located in the interiors of the blocks in order to maintain the street wall. The vast parking lots required for regional shopping centers are placed along collector roads as pedestrian activity is impossible there in any case. In these parking lots the traffic lanes are planned as an urban grid, to allow for the eventual replacement of parking by buildings as the town center matures.

Affordable housing is addressed with the goal of integrating it in small quantities throughout the neighborhood instead of creating large tracts of single-income housing. This can be achieved to a large degree by the following: 1) interspersing houses of different sizes but similar appearance; 2) providing apartments over stores; 3) encouraging garage apartments and small cottages behind single-family homes to serve as rental units.

Other growth management issues such as the balance of jobs and housing, school size and placement, and the equitable distribution of resources, all have a place in the above design principles.

The Charrette

The process of designing a town in a week-long charrette began with Seaside. This first attempt to create a complete town instead of a mixed-use development involved numerous participants. Subsequently, as the projects have become larger and more complex, often requiring elaborate approval processes, the charrette has provided a setting in which all constituents—from municipal officials to interested citizens—can participate in the planning process. The charrette helps to educate the participants, incorporate their contributions, verify decisions and diminish the adversities of the ensuing permitting process.

8

9

The charrette establishes a full working office of 5 to 20 people on site, staffed with a small core of experienced Duany and Plater-Zyberk designers, working with local architects, landscape architects, historians, engineers, ecologists, and financial and marketing consultants (*Figs. 8, 9*).

The charrette begins with a day of visits to the site and to nearby towns which might serve as models, and a presentation to the community of the principles of town planning. During the following days, the team, including the client, works day and night, meeting often with local officials and advocacy groups, designing everything from the master plan to typical buildings, the codes and specific landscapes.

Design authorship is exchanged for the authenticity of character that usually only history can give: different individuals work sequentially with entire schemes handed over to others to develop. The results, usually presented in a public slide lecture on the last evening, may include up to 40 drawings.

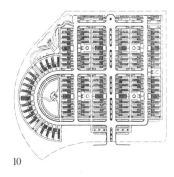

10

11

---

*William Lennertz is an architect
in practice with Duany and
Plater-Zyberk and a visiting design
critic at Harvard University
Graduate School of Design.*

Implementation

In the pre-Seaside project of Charleston Place, Duany and Plater-Zyberk discovered the limitations of current zoning codes on town planning. The creation of the traditional townhouse neighborhood of Charleston Place was possible only through a creative interpretation of the zoning code; the plan was permitted as a grid of "parking tracts" to avoid both the prohibition on driveways and excessive building setbacks *(Figs. 10, 11)*. Clever or lenient code interpretation, however, cannot circumvent single-minded engineering and planning standards, and conventional beliefs that only traffic flow, parking counts, and the segregation of uses are important—impediments to building according to traditional town patterns. Some communities are surprised to learn that the urban patterns of a historic district they wish to preserve are no longer allowed.

Repeated confrontations with municipal ordinances led to the development of the Traditional Neighborhood District Ordinance (TND). The ordinance can be tailored to specific needs and has been incorporated in the laws of communities in four states. Duany and Plater-Zyberk are currently working on the TUD (Traditional Urban District), an ordinance for retrofitting existing urban neighborhoods.

Selected Works

This catalogue is not a comprehensive exposition of the work of Duany and Plater-Zyberk or of any one project. Rather, it is a selection intended to show the range of solutions which their work brings to current planning and urban design problems. The drawings represent different stages in project development: some were produced "in charrette," while others can be considered final.

Illustrations

1–7
Duany and Plater-Zyberk's drawings of Seaside.

8, 9
The Kentlands project charrette.

10, 11
Duany and Plater-Zyberk's design for Charleston Place, Boca Raton, Florida.

Seaside

80 acres

Designed 1982

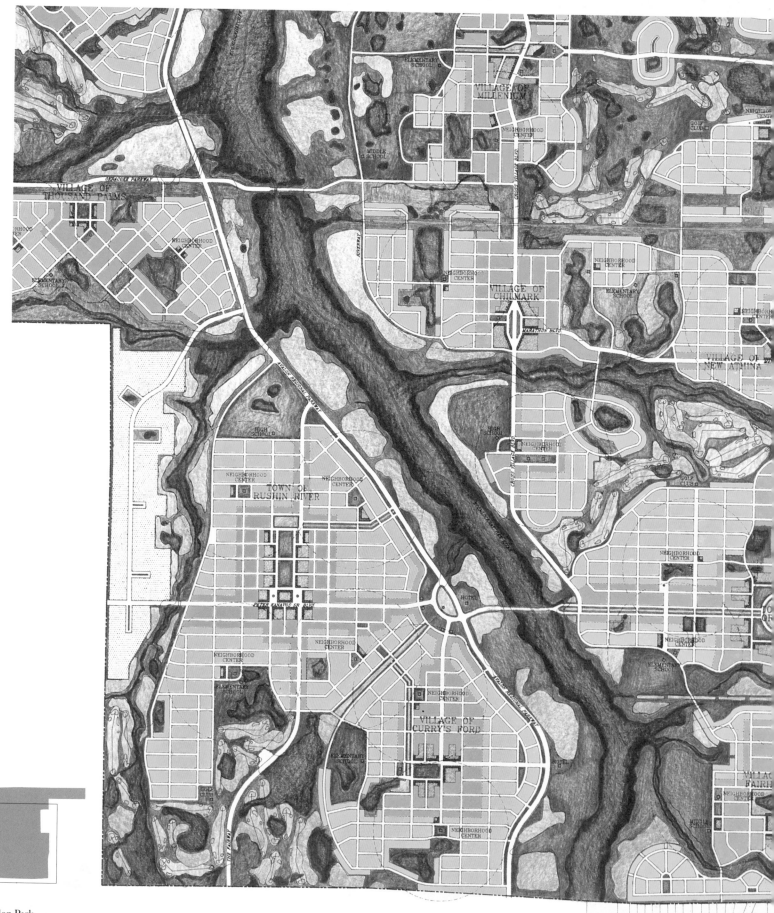

Avalon Park

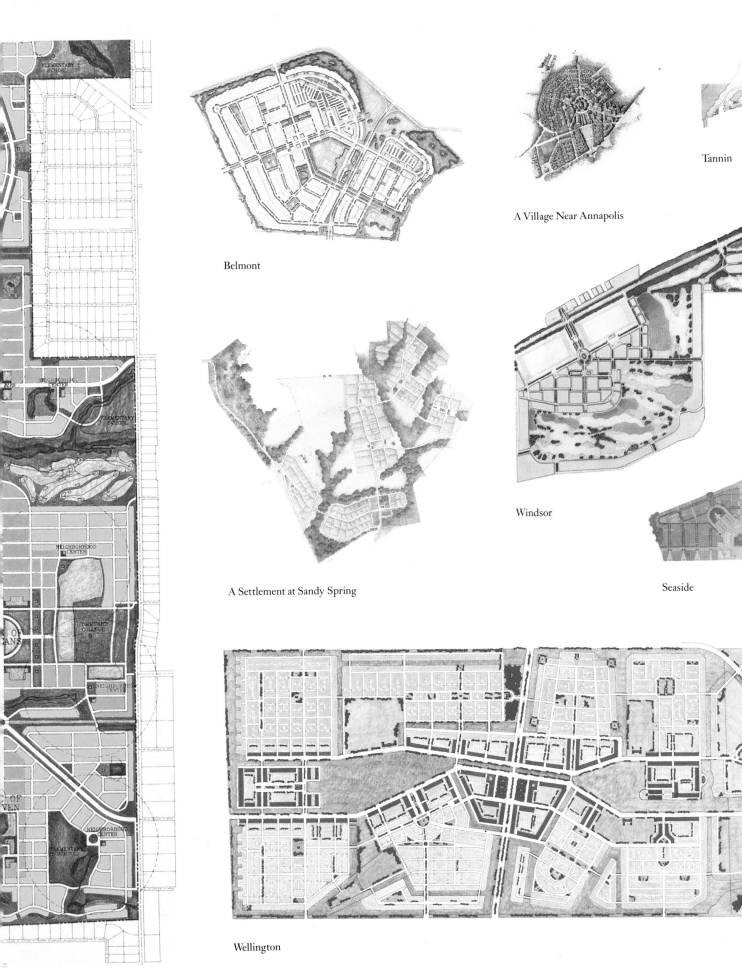

Belmont

A Village Near Annapolis

Tannin

A Settlement at Sandy Spring

Windsor

Seaside

Wellington

VILLAGES, TOWNS, CITIES, AND TERRITORIES

Scale: 1″ = 1850′

0   1850   3700

0   1350 = 5-minute walk

Kentlands

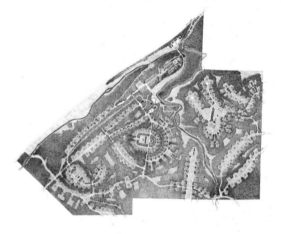

Blue Hole Village at Blount Springs

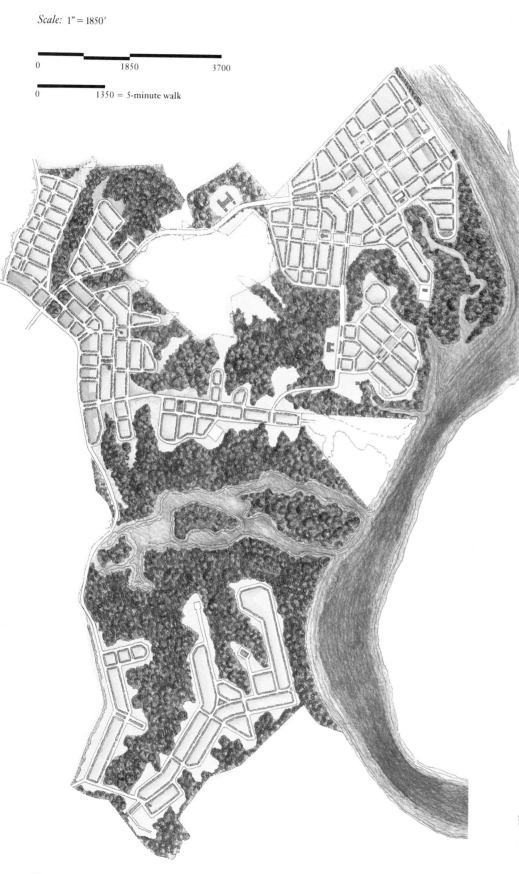

Haymount

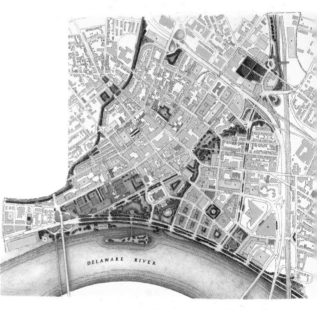

Capital City Renaissance

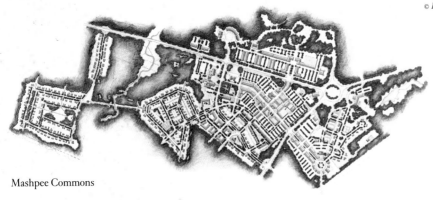

Mashpee Commons

Nance Canyon

Avalon Park

9,400 acres

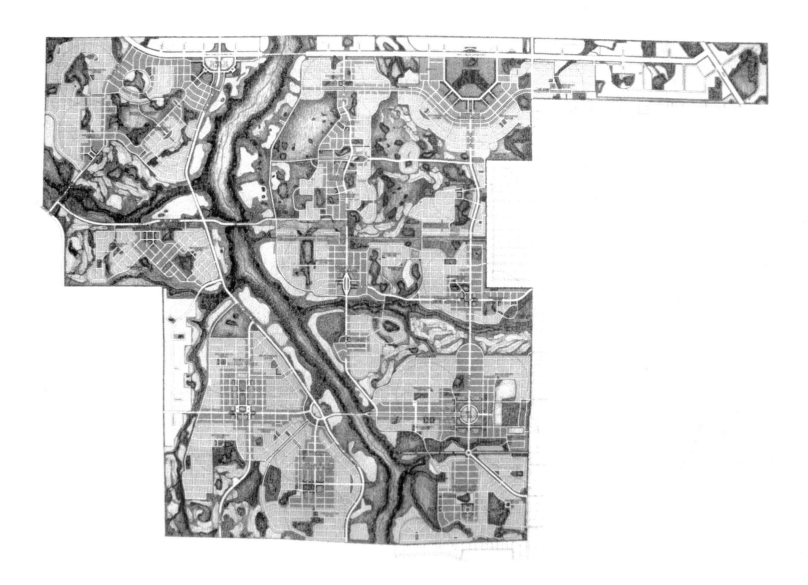

Designed 1989

VILLAGES

The history of a nation is only a history of its villages written large.

Woodrow Wilson, 1900

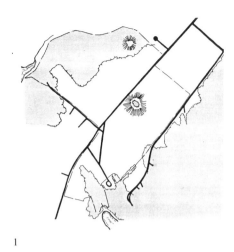

1

A VILLAGE NEAR ANNAPOLIS

Anne Arundel County, Maryland

While, therefore, he must recognize the beauty of curved roads, he must resist the temptation to produce aimlessly wandering lines, in the hope that happy accidents may result therefrom.

Raymond Unwin, 1909

A rural village

A mixture of residential, institutional, and commercial uses is intended to serve a community of all ages, with special attention to the needs of senior citizens. A retirement home is located close to the center allowing its residents easy access to community activities. The home includes the village cinema to further encourage interaction among older and younger community residents.

Like that of nearby Annapolis, this plan radiates from a hilltop circle where the meeting hall stands as the terminus for each uphill street view. The streets have sidewalks and a system of pedestrian paths cut through the blocks to maintain short walking distances. There are several small squares with adjacent lots reserved for public buildings. Other public facilities include a market square lined by shops, community gardens which use an existing barn for tool storage, a place of worship, and a cemetery.

Private land is platted in 15-, 30-, 40-, and 60-foot lots. To accommodate all age groups, the code specifies five dwelling types: courtyard apartment buildings, apartments above shops, townhouses, side-yard houses, and detached houses with rental outbuildings.

2

Owner's name withheld

174 acres
487 dwelling units
80,000 sf commercial/office
Retirement home
Meeting hall
Place of worship
Post office
Library
Park pavilions
Allotment gardens
Cemetery

Designed February 1988
Redesigned by others

1
A drawing of the existing conditions. The site lies along a rural road that ends nearby at the Chesapeake Bay. Two hills distinguish the geography. On the most prominent of these is to be the village center.

2
The existing road is to be diverted to run through the property and the village center, which will then benefit from the energizing economic effect of through traffic.

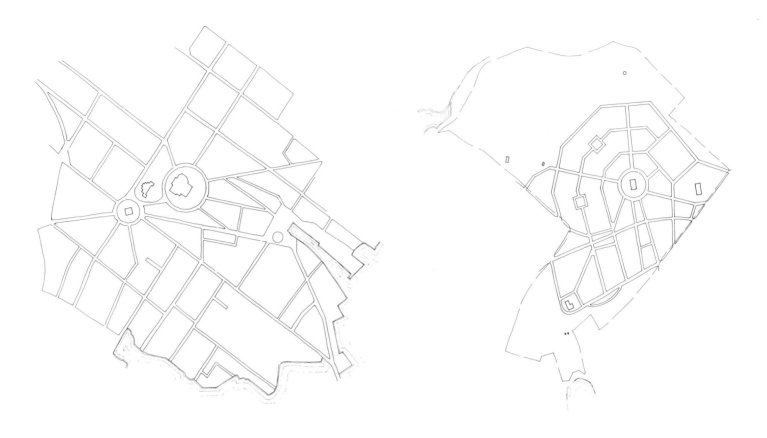

3
Modeled on Francis Nicholson's plan for Annapolis, the new village places its primary public building in a circle on the highest ground.

4
Neighborhood squares are flanked on two sides by public buildings and on two sides by private residences. Greens and squares have decisive shapes that read as outdoor public rooms.

5
A public pavilion atop the second hill is the gateway to the park along the creek.

4

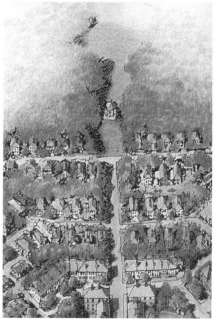

5

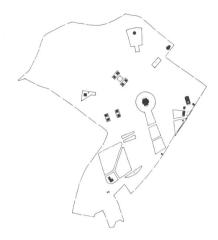

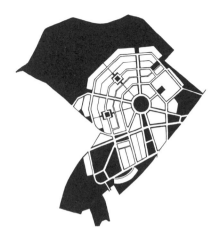

6

Sites reserved for public buildings are distributed throughout the village. Most are located at squares.

7

The web-shaped plan combines characteristics of two grid types: the intelligibility of the orthogonal and the efficiency of the radial.

8

The pedestrian network includes parks, squares, sidewalks along streets, and walkways cutting through the blocks. This network links all parts of the plan, making walking throughout the village easier than driving.

9

The village plan.

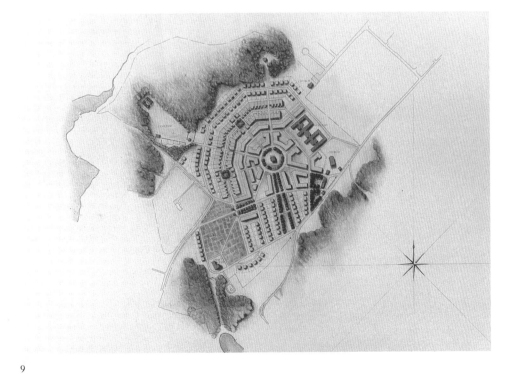

9

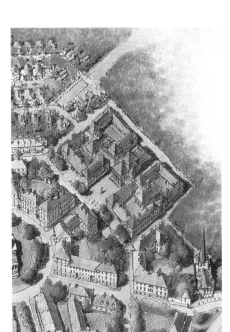

10

The retirement home occupies a small campus with several courtyard buildings.

10

29

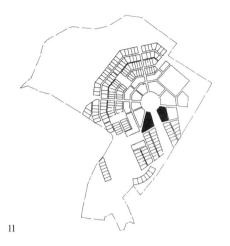
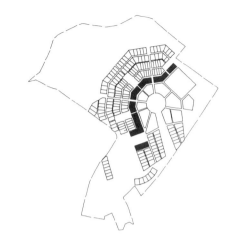
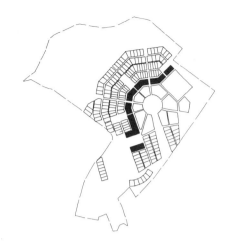

11

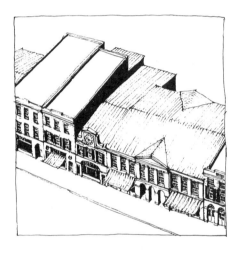

12

Type I. Shopfronts with commercial uses on the ground floor and offices on the upper floors.

Type II. Row houses with door yards.

Type IIa. Row houses with porches.

11
Five building types are delineated by the Urban Code. The diagrams show their proximity in plan, which promotes an integration of income levels.

12
The five building types are time-proven and flexible and may be mixed successfully along adjacent streets. A limited series of types can respond to a variety of needs.

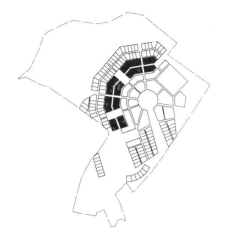

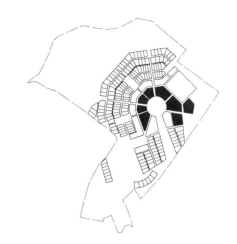

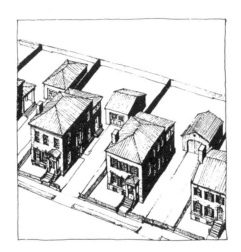

Type III. Sideyard houses, which may be duplexes.

Type IV. Detached single family houses with out-
buildings.

Type V. Courtyard apartment buildings.

A SETTLEMENT AT SANDY SPRING

Sandy Spring, Maryland

1

The country town is one of the great American insitutions; perhaps the greatest,
in the sense that it has had a greater part than any other in shaping public
sentiment and giving character to American culture.

Thorstein Veblin, 1922

Rural villages and greenbelt

This project proposes the compact rural village as an alternative to low-density suburban
sprawl. The site is adjacent to a traditional one-street Maryland town called Sandy Spring.
Every Sunday, Quaker residents of the town cross the project site en route to their
meeting, passing the spring from which the town takes its name.

Recognizing the community's concern for the land, the design team developed an
initial plan in compliance with the existing two-acre zoning, and two alternative plans for
compact villages. Local residents and officials reviewed these plans. The entitlement plan
required the privatization of virtually all of the site with large expensive homes. The
village plans allowed for a variety of densities and unit sizes, and provided open fields and
woods between the villages. Participating citizens assisted in selecting one of the latter for
development.

Observation of nearby towns such as New Market and Burkitsville revealed four
different approaches to placing houses along public spaces. The urban code for Sandy
Spring, therefore, dictates the placement of buildings according to whether they front a
square, a street, lane, or road, with few other restrictions on building type.

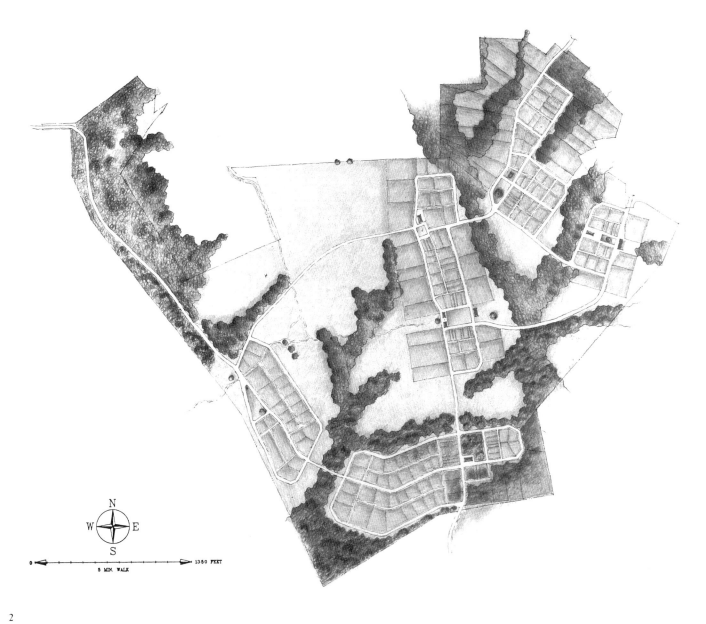

N
W · E
S

0 — 1350 FEET
5 MIN. WALK

2

Joseph Alfandre & Company, Inc.

400 acres
225 dwelling units
Meeting hall
4 corner stores
Allotment gardens

Designed September 1988
Permits pending

1
An aerial view of the Sandy Spring site.

2
The final charrette plan shows villages surrounding
a heath which protects the Sandy Spring.

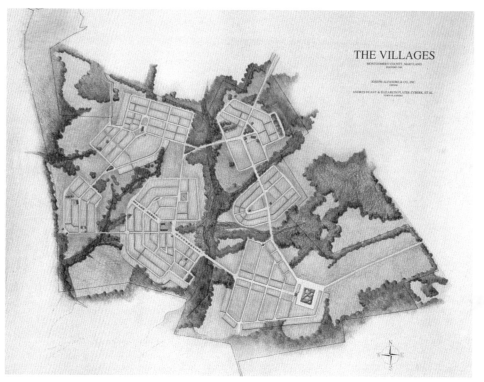

3

3

The first charrette plan has six villages separated by greenbelts. Each village has a center green with a corner store as well as a site for a meeting hall.

4

A detail of the first charrette plan.

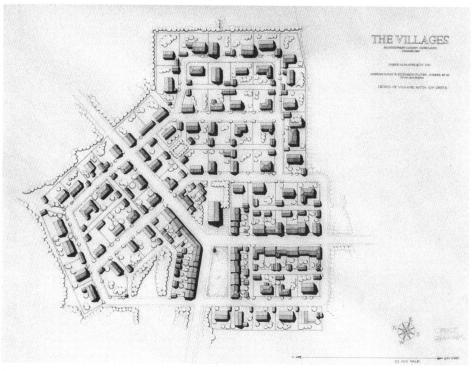

4

5

A view of Sandy Spring from the approach shows a village surrounded by open farmland.

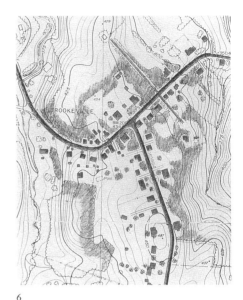

6

A plan of Brooksville, Maryland, a nearby cross-road village, which served as a model.

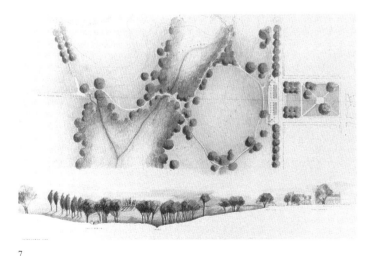

7

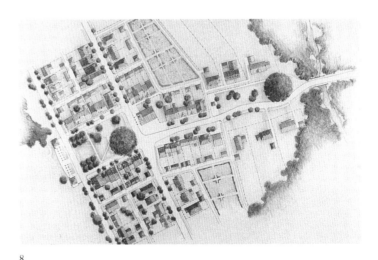

8

7

Detail of a square designed by Warren Byrd and the heath overlooking the spring.

8

The village center showing the mix of building types around the public square.

A TYPICAL STREET

A TYPICAL LANE

A TYPICAL ROAD

9

Sandy Spring has a hierarchy of streets, lanes, and roads. These types relate not to traffic capacity but to the gradation from the more urban center to its more rural edges. Lot sizes and housing types may be mixed in the manner of traditional villages, which bring together a population of various economic means.

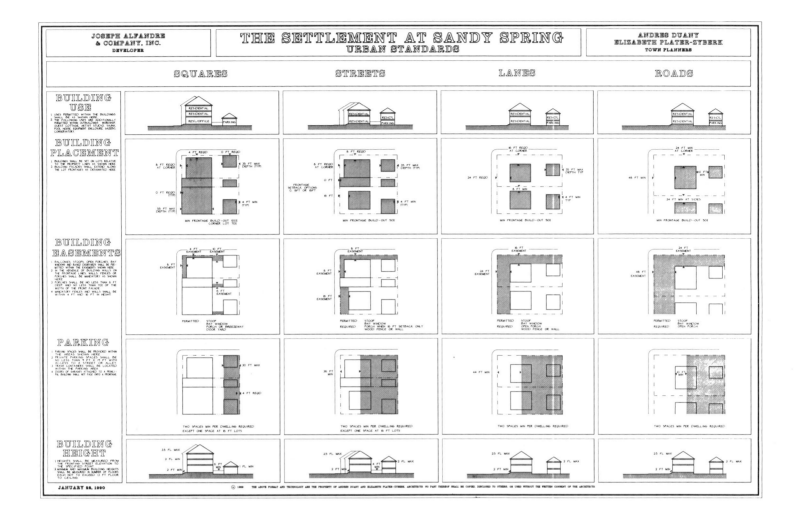

10

The Urban Standards for Sandy Spring are unusual because they are categorized by location on square, street, lane or road. The code dictates the disposition of the building and the placement of parking but leaves building types varied. This flexibility encourages the irregularity characteristic of village urbanism.

WINDSOR

Vero Beach, Florida

1

The classical idiom does not so much impose unity, as make diversity agreeable.

Roger Scruton, 1984

A village of unified architectural expression

Windsor is a resort village on Florida's east coast. The heart of the village is a neighborhood of intimate scale designed in the urban tradition of the Caribbean. A golf course and polo fields surround this central neighborhood.

Windsor is designed to function as a real community. At its center is the market crescent, a two-story building which includes a general store, post office, restaurant, cafe, offices, an inn, and apartments. The market crescent serves as both a gateway to the community and a focus for its daily life. Other community facilities are within walking distance of the crescent, including the meeting hall and the beach, tennis, and golf clubs.

The urban regulations require houses and continuous garden walls to be built at the property lines, defining the streets and squares of the village and forming private gardens. The architectural regulations mandate the vernacular architecture of the region with first floors of masonry, wood construction above, and porches, balconies, and roof overhangs. With the exception of the Poundbury Code, this is the most precise of Duany and Plater-Zyberk's small town codes. Windsor will be architecturally harmonious to a high degree.

Streets vary in size and character, from the broad entrance boulevard—flanked by allees of trees and leading to the market crescent—to small neighborhood streets. Generally, north-south streets measure 48 feet in width and east-west streets are 28 feet across.

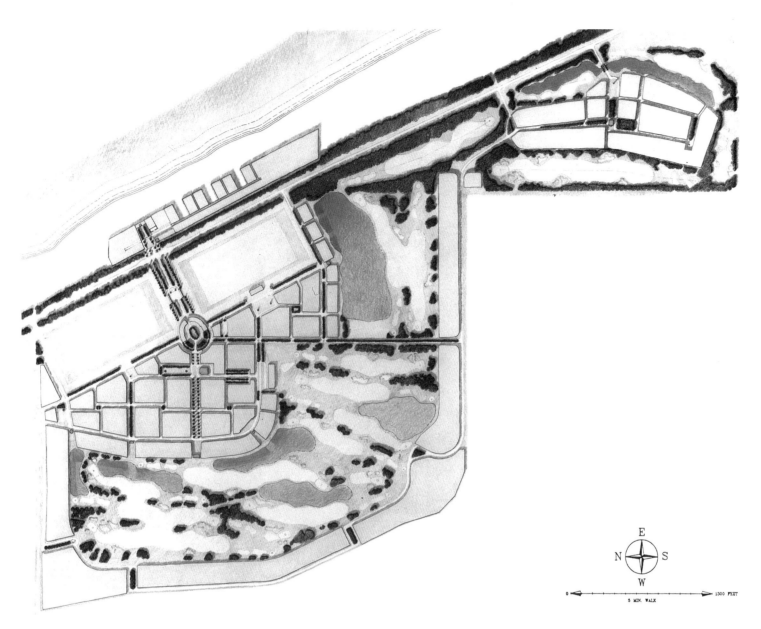

2

N E S W

0 |————————| 1300 FEET
5 MIN. WALK

Galen and Hilary Weston
Geoffrey and Jorie Kent

400 acres
320 dwelling units
8-room inn
Meeting hall
Post office
General store
Beach club
Golf club

Designed May 1989
Under construction

1
Windsor is sited between the Atlantic Ocean and the Inland Waterway in Vero Beach, Florida.

2
Windsor's village center is situated along Route A1A behind two existing polo fields. These form a greenbelt along the regional road. At the center of the village a market building organizes the plan.

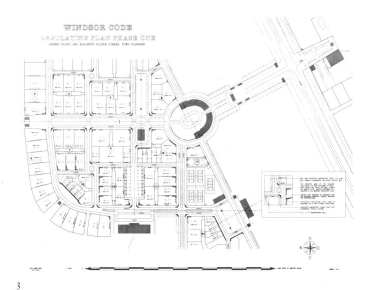

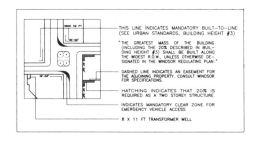

3

A detail of the Regulating Plan keyed to the Urban Standards that control building type and define street space.

4

5

4

A Type II building under construction at Windsor. Architect, Scott Merrill.

5

The Urban Standards for Windsor form tight street spaces by requiring buildings and garden walls to be placed close to the street. This is the first of three sheets.

6

A view of the Crescent at the village center.

7

A view of the meeting hall on the green.

8

A drawing showing the layout of narrow streets and courtyards for a typical block.

9

A view of a Windsor street, twenty-eight feet from building to building, with the overhanging balconies and foliage of the private courtyards.

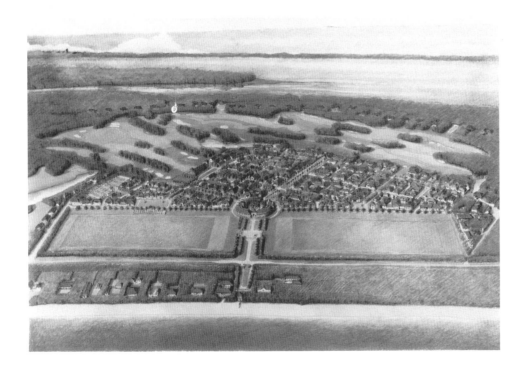

10

A drawing of the village center.

TANNIN

Orange Beach, Alabama

1

I had the great good fortune to have been raised in a small town.

Dwight D. Eisenhower

A coastal village

Tannin is located on the north shore of the Gulf of Mexico. The plan for Tannin responds to several awkward site characteristics including an irregular property boundary and a linear dune and wetland formation which lies oblique to the highway. The street grid runs parallel to this topographic feature.

The wetlands within the site have become linear lakes, while the swamp to the north and west of the site remain wild, overlooked by residential lots and by a public pavilion which terminates the main boulevard. A town square at the highway provides sites for commercial buildings, as well as a village hall, post office, and regional fire station. This concentration of civic activities will function as the center of an area greater than Tannin.

Tannin's urban regulations prescribe the physical ingredients of traditional Southern building types; the architectural regulations specify construction materials and techniques that are economical and found in the local vernacular.

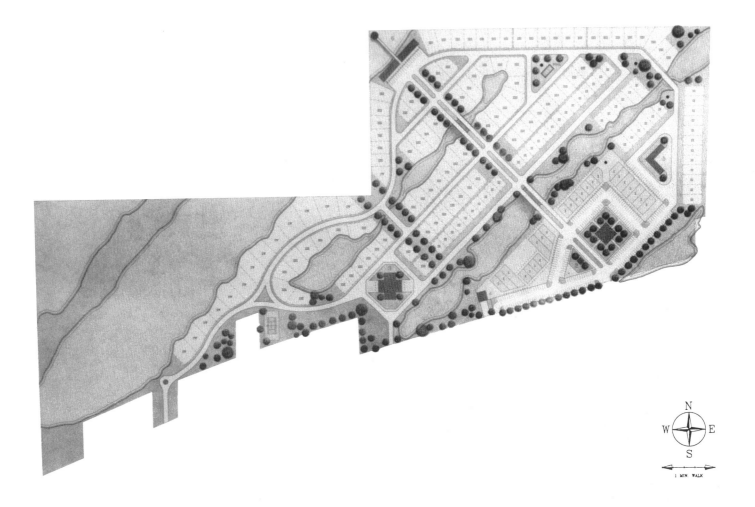

2

Tannin, Inc.
George Gounares
Joseph Burland

60 acres
172 dwelling units
40,000 sf commercial
25 room inn
Village hall
Place of worship
Post office
Fire station
Crafts center

Designed July 1986
Under construction

1
Existing conditions at Tannin.

2
The master plan for Tannin showing the street grid parallel to the canals and the town center along the state highway.

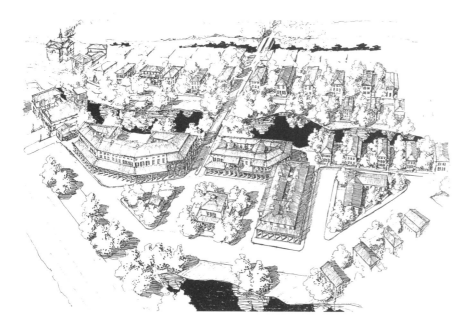

3

An aerial perspective of the town center.

4

A Type II house under construction.

5

A Type III house viewed from the canal.

6

The Urban Code regulates five building types: a town center shopfront with apartments above, a sideyard house, two different types of detached houses, and a bungalow court.

4

5

URBAN CODE
THE VILLAGE OF TANNIN

6

T O W N S   A N D   C I T I E S

There can be no doubt . . . that, in all our modern civilization, as in that of the ancients, there is a strong drift townward.

Frederick Law Olmsted, 1877

1

BELMONT

Loudoun County, Virginia

Although it might seem at first glance that the picturesque maze of a medieval town could interest only a painter or an enthusiast for old masonry, an attentive scrutiny of the disposition of streets will not be without benefit even to the modern technical expert.

Camillo Sitte, 1889

A town with flexible platting

Belmont is situated near Leesburg, Virginia, in a rural area of Loudoun County characterized by rolling hills, farms, and villages. Recently, the county initiated strict controls on growth in response to suburban Washington's sprawl. With its own landscape as a model, the county has proposed a village and greenbelt structure for future development, incorporating the Traditional Neighborhood Development Ordinance into its zoning legislation under the name Rural Village Ordinance.

The plan for Belmont was influenced by two of Loudoun's historic towns, Waterford, and Leesburg where the charrette team was quartered. Leesburg's street grid, which has accommodated two centuries of growth, provides a model for town design with flexibility for future evolution. Belmont's residential streets, like those of the historic town, have a controlled variation of building setbacks.

The combination of building types and sizes observed in Waterford provides a model for the intermingling of housing of varying costs. Towards this end, the Belmont plan appropriates the colonial American method of platting private property in rods—lot frontage increments of approximately 16 feet—which allows a variety of lot aggregations, both large and small, on the same street. This platting system has become normative in subsequent plans. It fits current building types exceptionally well and, at the aggregate of 64 feet, can be a recurring parking module.

Belmont's neighborhoods are organized around greens and civic buildings, including a school, a town hall, and several churches. The town center is internal due to the requirement for a buffer along the county road.

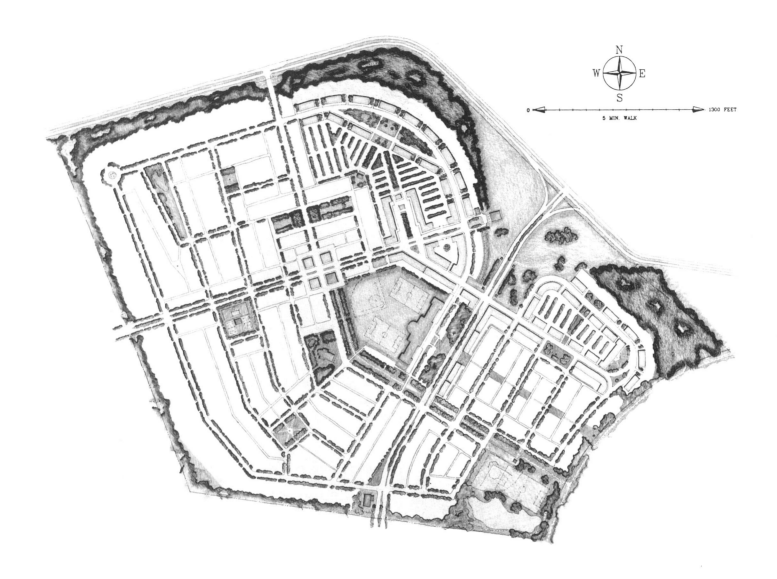

2

1
An aerial view of the site.

2
The master plan shows the workplace and shopping area along the highway, the school at the center, several neighborhoods organized around greens, and the corner of a regional park which is shared with adjacent properties.

Joseph Alfandre & Company, Inc.

273 acres
752 dwelling units
365,000 sf office
163,000 sf commercial
Town hall
2 places of worship
2 elementary schools
Child care facility

Designed September 1988
Under construction

3

4

3
The site with Leesburg superimposed for a scale comparison.

4
Public buildings—town hall, churches, schools, and childcare facilities — are sited on greens or at the ends of important streets, where they serve to terminate views.

5
The town center.

5

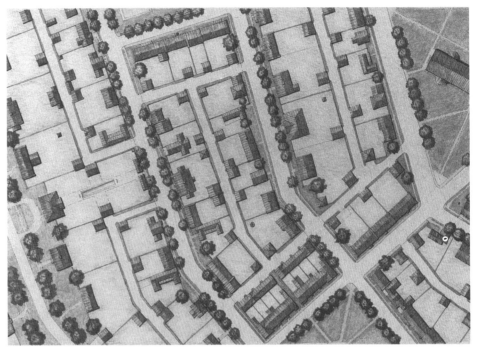

6

6

A plan detail shows various options for the division of land into lots. The smallest lots are near the town center; the largest lots are at the edges. Buildings, walls, or fences are aligned along varying build-to lines to shape the street. If a homeowner chooses not to build on the line, a fence must be substituted for the building wall.

7

Linden Square, designed by Jay Graham.

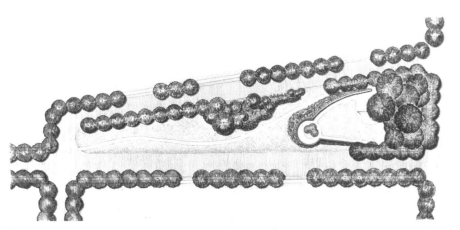

7

8

The street network is a distorted grid influenced by the plan of Leesburg. Street connections to adjacent developments link the town to the regional circulation network.

9

Belmont was platted using the rod. The rod is a colonial American measure of approximately sixteen feet, a module still appropriate to the current housing market. Land is sold in multiples of this increment, allowing a variety of lot sizes along any given street.

10

Street elevations showing the variety of building types and sizes possible on a commercial street and on a residential street.

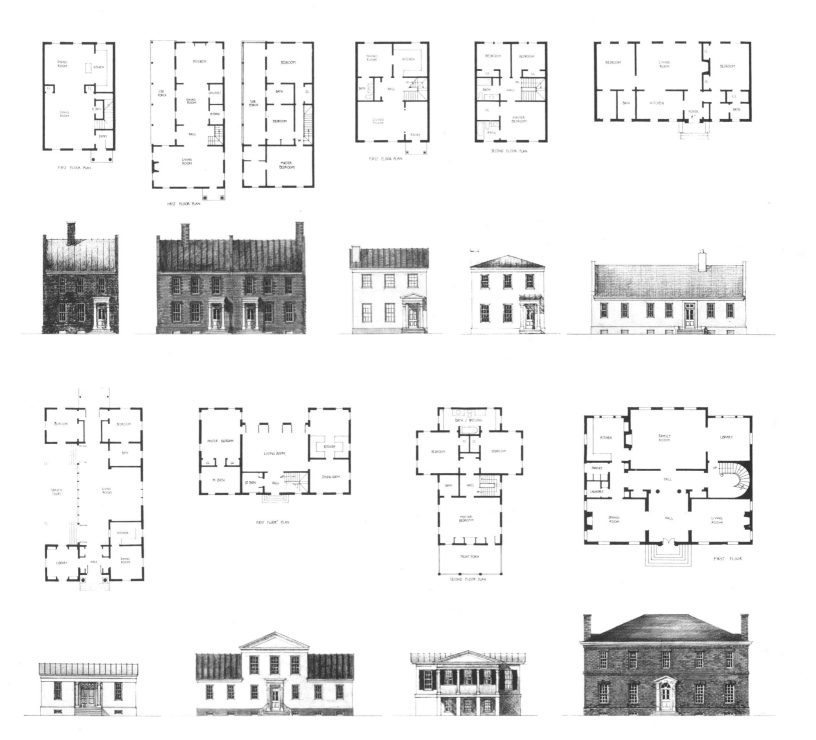

11

Some of the Virginia building types envisioned
during the creation of the Code.

KENTLANDS

Gaithersburg, Maryland

1

A year ago, the Gallup Organization asked people if they prefer to live in a city, suburb, small town, or farm. Small towns were the choice favored by 34 percent; 24 percent chose a suburb; 22 percent preferred a farm and 19 percent favored a city. Four out of five respondents lived in a metropolitan area.

New York Times, Sept. 11, 1990

Incorporating a shopping center into a town

The Kent Farm site is surrounded by conventional suburban office parks, townhouse subdivisions, and strip shopping centers. The property was zoned for mixed uses with the intention that it provide a commercial center for the region.

In response to the requirement to make the Kentlands commercial component a regional shopping center, a series of designs was developed over a two-and-a-half-year period attempting to hybridize this distinct and inflexible type with a traditional downtown. One constant has been maintained: the evolving scheme is seamlessly attached to the street grid of the Kentlands neighborhoods in such a way that residents will conveniently walk into the center of town from the four neighborhoods.

The town square, at the heart of the Midtown neighborhood, is bordered by a church, the shopping center entrance, and four-story buildings which contain shops, offices, and apartments. Midtown is connected by a regular street grid to the Old Farm neighborhood.

Old Farm is centered on the original Kent homestead, which is to be the town's cultural arts center. The new streets are arranged irregularly as an extension of the informal siting of the house and barns.

The Hill District neighborhood overlooks Old Farm and its lake, and is centered on a community clubhouse. Hill streets run diagonally up the contours to minimize their impact on the slopes.

The School District neighborhood focuses on a circle ringed by the elementary school, a church, a corner store, a child care facility, and a row of townhouses. Here a pattern of straight streets follows the gently sloping open landscape.

2

Joseph Alfandre & Company, Inc.

356 acres
1600 dwelling units
1 million sf office
1.2 million sf commercial
Meeting house
2 places of worship
Library
Elementary school
Child care facility
Recreational club house

Designed June 1988
Under construction

1
The Kent Farm, Gaithersburg, Maryland.

2
The plan of Kentlands.

4

5

3
The School District includes a new elementary school, a church, a corner store, a child care facility and a row of townhouses.

4, 5
The first buildings in the School District.

6

7

8

6
The Old Farm Neighborhood encompasses the existing Kent estate. The original estate buildings will house a cultural center for Kentlands and Gaithersburg, and will include artists' lofts, a conference center, a post office, public gardens, and a restaurant.

7
Old and new buildings in the Old Farm Neighborhood.

8
The Hill District has parallel streets that gently climb the grade of the hill.

The following series of drawings and sketches represents the design development of the town center and its adjacent regional shopping center.

9, 10
Prior to the charrette, the independent retail developer agreed to a hybrid shopping center plan, to serve both a regional clientele arriving by car and neighborhood residents arriving on foot. The shopping center is integrated into the town by attaching its anchor stores to the main street, thus allowing pedestrian access which avoids traversing parking lots.

11, 12
During the charrette, the retail developer demanded a more conventional shopping center plan. The charrette yielded a new plan which joins the shopping center to Midtown at the square only. The plan shows this scheme in progress. The rendering shows the charrette's final presentation scheme.

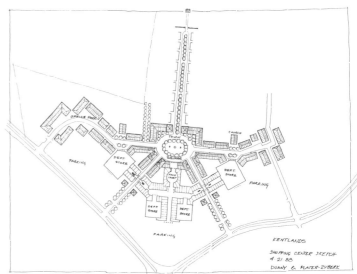

9

10

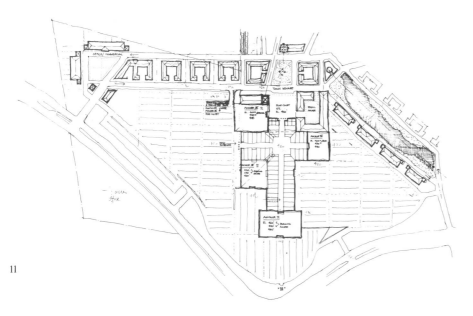

11

12

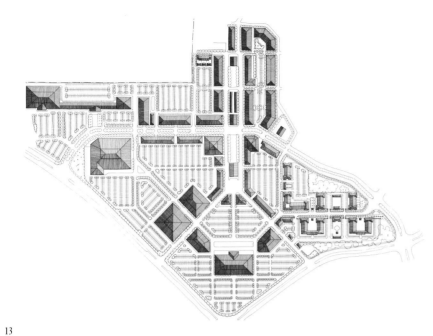

13

14

15

13

A post-charrette plan by Duany and Plater-Zyberk with Eskew-Filson Architects. The town square extends into the shopping center.

14

A post-charrette plan by Duany and Plater-Zyberk with Design International. Town streets lined with stores extend through the parking lots toward the anchor stores positioned near the highway.

15

A more recent proposal for the shopping center by Aldo Rossi and Morris Adjmi.

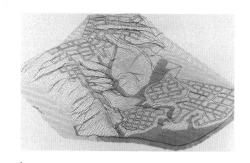

1

HAYMOUNT

Caroline County, Virginia

Americans love their towns for much the same reasons that highlanders love their mountains. In both cases the native land has emphatic and peculiar features; it has a more pronounced physiognomy than is found elsewhere.

Alexis de Tocqueville, 1833

A river town

The site of Haymount lies along the Rappahannock River in Virginia. Hilly terrain and wetlands outline the buildable areas and organize the plan into neighborhoods surrounded by parks.

The principal neighborhood, adjacent to the river, is designed on a grid similar to that of Leesburg, Virginia, adapted to the natural conditions of the site. The street system is designed to connect in the future to several outparcels which are within the general outline of the parcel.

Four square blocks straddle the main streets, and linear blocks make up the rest of the urban fabric. The square blocks enclose common parking which is required by the higher density buildings of the main street. The linear blocks, which make up the outlying areas, easily accommodate individual houses with their individual parking.

A landing defined by commercial buildings joins the town to the river. Additional squares are provided for civic buildings—at least one for each neighborhood.

Haymount's landscape design varies from formal and manicured at the town squares to controlled nature in the parks, to undisturbed nature at the periphery. Lots at neighborhood edges have special landscaping requirements to help them blend with the natural surroundings.

Haymount Limited Partnership, owner
Robertson and Clark, developers

1,582 acres
4,000+ dwelling units
50,000 sf office
250,000 sf commercial
12 places of worship
High school
Elementary school

Designed December 1989
Permits pending

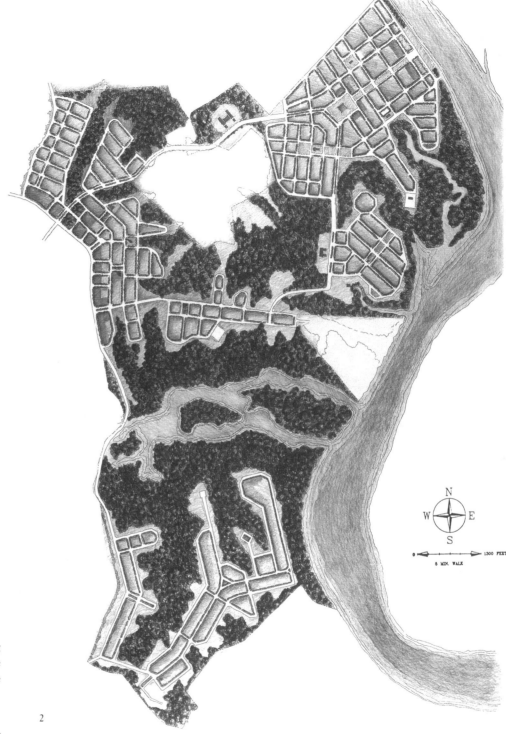

1

A computer-generated drawing produced during the charrette. While the plan is influenced by the topography, streets do not necessarily follow the contours.

2

2

Haymount has five neighborhoods of different character determined by the topographical conditions. The riverside neighborhood has a promenade park lined with shops. The roadside neighborhood contains the extension campus of a local college and the major commercial development.

3, 4

Two of the many plans sketched on the first day of the charrette.

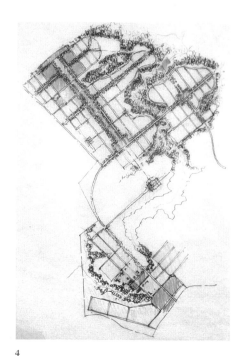

3

4

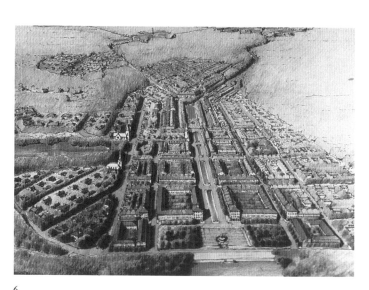

5

6

5, 6

Two aerial views of Haymount, one looking from and the other toward the river.

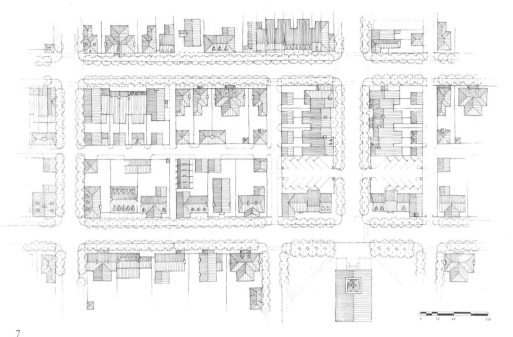

7

8

7

A drawing of a neighborhood showing a variety of building types in combination and the flexible lot arrangement that encourages variety.

8

A study showing a block of small cottages and out-buildings on some of the larger house lots. Each cottage is no larger than an efficiency apartment. They allow people with varied incomes — service workers, students, or senior citizens — to share the amenities of a neighborhood while the homeowner benefits from renting the cottage.

9

The public promenade as seen from the river.

9

10

11

10

A neighborhood center consisting of a green surrounded by buildings with shops on the first floor and offices or apartments above. The bus stops here.

11

A street showing two options for setbacks.

12

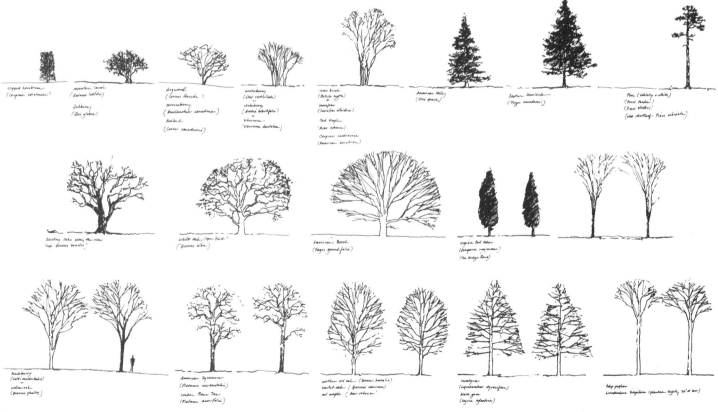

13

HAYMOUNT LIMITED PARTNERSHIP OWNER ROBERTSON & CLARK DEVELOPER	THE HAYMOUNT CODE LIST OF NATIVE PLANTS	ANDRES DUANY ELIZABETH PLATER-ZYBERK TOWN PLANNERS

PLANTING ON PUBLIC TRACTS

- All trees in public tracts shall have a minimum of 2 1/2" -3" caliper with a 16'-18' height (B&B). These trees shall limb up a minimum of 8' above ground line.
- Avenue and boulevard trees shall have a minimum 4 1/2" - 5" caliper, with a 22'- 24' height. These trees shall limb up a minimum of 10' above ground line.

1. LARGE SQUARES & PARKS

Primary tree should be white oak (Quercus alba)

On the grounds of civic buildings include/consider:
Quercus phellos (Willow Oak)
Quercus coccinea (Scarlet Oak)
Quercus falcata (Southern Red Oak)
Liriodendron tulipifera (Tulip Poplar)
Fagus grandifolia (American Beech)
Quercus phellos (Willow Oak)

In parks also include/consider:
Acer rubrum (Red Maple)
Nyssa sylvatica (Black Gum)
Liquidambar styraciflua (Sweetgum)
Cornus florida (Flowering Dogwood)
Cercis canddensis (Redbud)
Amelanchies canadensis (Serviceberry)
Magnolia virginiana (Sweetbay)

2. SMALL RESIDENTIAL SQUARES

Trees: (24' spacing on center)
(selection depends on streets)
Fraxinus americana (White Ash)
Platanus acerifolia (London-Plane)
Quercus coccinea (Scarlet Oak)
Nyssa sylvatica (Black gum)
Acer rubrum (Red Maple)

3. AVENUE

Trees: (spacing 24', 32', 40', 48' on center)
Quercus phellos (Willow Oak)
Liriodendron tulipifera (Tulip Poplar)
Fagus grandifolia (American Beech)

4. BOULEVARD

Trees: (spacing 24', 32', 40', 48' on center)
Quercus phellos (Willow Oak)
Liriodendron tulipifera (Tulip Poplar)
Fagus grandifolia (American Beech)

5. LARGE STREET

Trees: (spacing 24' on center)
Acer rubrum (Red Maple)
Nyssa sylvatica (Black Gum)

6. SMALL STREET

Trees (spacing 24' - 40' on center)
Celtis occidentalis (Hackberry)
Quercus coccinea (Scarlet Oak)
Quercus borealis (Northern Red Oak)

7. DRIVE

Upland Trees (spacing 24' or 48' on center)
Fagus grandifolia (American Beech)
Liriodendron tulipifera (tulip poplar)
Quercus coccinea (Scarlet Oak)
Quercus borealis (Northern Red Oak)

Wetland Trees: (spacing 24' or 48' on center)
Celtis occidentalis - Hackberry
Platanus occidentalis (native)- American Sycamore
Liquidambar styraciflua- sweetgum
Acer rubrum - Red Maple

8. ROADS

Trees: (spacing variable : min. 8'; max. 64')
Quercus phellos (Willow Oak)
Quercus Coccinea (Scarlet Oak)
Quercus borealis (Northern Red Oak)

Smaller Trees: (spacing variable : min. 4'-max. 16')
Sassafras albidum (Sassafras)
Cornus Florida (Flowering Dogwood)
Cercis canadensis (Eastern Redbud)

*non-native

PLANTING ON PUBLIC LOTS

- Existing trees over 6" in caliper shall not be removed except with the permission of the Town Architect's office.
- There shall be at least one tree of the species listed below (on not less than 3 1/2" caliper) planted in a front or rear yard for each 16' of street frontage.
- The use of native species of trees, shrubs, vines, groundcovers and perennials is encouraged in order to make gardens compatible with the existing wildlife habitat and its regional context.
- The use of fruit, berry and nut trees is encouraged in order to contribute to the existing wildlife habitat.
- Planting of fruit trees in groups of four or greater (regularly spaced) is encouraged to create small orchards.
- Planting of nut trees in regular or irregularly-spaced groups of three or more is encouraged
- All shrubs should be planted in groups of at least three (of like species) rather than as individuals. (Minimum spacing - 2 feet on center for hedges...up to 5' on center maximum for open plantings.)
- Plantings in immediate proximity to buildings should respect architectural lines (that is, should be seen as extensions of the architectural walls), whereas plantings toward the backs of yards could take on more irregular and "naturalized" configurations and spacings.
- Plantings toward the street should respect the integrity of the street. Plantings should not obscure the buildings and should respect views to and from streets, porches, walks and public parks.

1. DECIDUOUS CANOPY TREES

Quercus phellos (Willow Oak)
Q. alba (White Oak)
Q. coccinea (Scarlet Oak)
Q. borealis (Norther Red Oak)
Q. falcata (Southern Red Oak)
Fagus grandifolia (American Beech)
* Castanea mollissima (Chinese Chestnut)
Nyssa sylvatica (Black Gum)
Acer rubrum (Red Maple)
Fraxinus americana (White Ash)
Celtis occidentalis (Hackberry)
Liquidambar styraciflua (Sweetgum)
Platanus occidentalis (Sycamore)
Liriodendron tulipifera (Tulip Poplar)

2. MEDIUM DECIDUOUS SUBCANOPY TREES

Acer rubrum (Red Maple)
Betula nigra (River Birch)
Diospyrus virginiana (Persimmon)
Carpinus caroliniana (American Hornbeam)
Sassafras albidum (Sassafras)

3. SMALL FLOWERING UNDERSTORY TREES

Cornus florida (Flowering dogwood)
Cercis canadensis (Eastern Redbud)
Amelanchier canadensis (Serviceberry)
Magnolia virginiana (Sweetbay Magnolia)
Oxydendron arboreum (Sourwood)
Chionanthus virginicus (Fringe tree)
Viburnum nudiflorum (Pinkster Bloom)
Stewartia (Stewartia)
Malus (Crabapples)
* Lagerstroemia indica (Crape Myrtle)

4. FRUIT & NUT TREES

*Malus (Apple)
*Prunus persica (Peach)
*Prunus (Plums)
*Pyrus communis (Common Pear, Kiefer Pear)
Juglans nigra (Black Walnut)
Carya illinoiensis (Pecan)
*Castanea mollissima (Chinese Chestnut)
Quercus species (Oaks)
Fagus grandifolia (American Beech)
*Juglans regia (English Walnut)
Carya (Hickories)
Diospyrus virginiana (Persimmon)

5. EVERGREEN TREES

Tsuga canadensis (Eastern Hemlock)
Pinus strobus (White Pine)
Pinus echinata (Shortleaf Pine)
Ilex opaca (American Holly)
Pinus taeda (Loblolly)
Magnolia grandiflora (Southern Magnolia)

6. EVERGREEN SHRUBS

Kalmia latifolia (Mountain Laurel)
Ilex glabra (Inkberry)
Wax-myrtle (Wax-myrtle)
Rhododendron catawbiense (Catawba Rhododendron)
R. carolineanum (Carolina Rhododendron)
*Buxus sempervirens (American Boxwood)
*Buxus suffruticosa (English Boxwood)
*Azalea (Kurume Azalea hybrids)

7. DECIDUOUS SHRUBS

Ilex verticillata (Winterberry)
Viburnum dentatum (Arrowwood)
Viburnum species (native)
Aronia arbutifolia (Red Chokeberry)
Lindera benzoin (Spicebery)
Clethra alnifolia (Sweet Pepperbush)
Rhododendron nudiflorum (Pinxter Bloom)
Sambucus canadensis (Elderberry)
Vaccinium (Blueberries)

8. VINES

Clematis virginiana
Clematis paniculata
Clematis jackmanii
Parthenocissus quinquefolia (Virginia creeper)
Campsis radicans (Trumpet creeper)
Celastrus scandens (Bittersweet)
*Wisteria sinensis (wisteria, chinese)

9. EVERGREEN GROUNDCOVER

*Vinca minor (periwinkle)
*Vinca major (long-leaf Periwinkle)
*Hedera helix (English Ivy)
*Pachysandra terminalis (Pachysandra)
*Linope muscari (liriope)
*Ophiopogon japonicus (Mondo-grass)
*Hypericum calycinum (St. Johns Wort)
*Cotoneaster (Rockspray)
*Azalea sasuki "Gumpo" (gumpo azalea - dwarf)

10. WILD FLOWERS & FIELD FLOWERS

Woodland:
Bluebells
Iris
Columbine
Ladyslipper
Trillium
Mayapple
Ferns
Bloodroot
Hepatica
Troutlily
Spring Beauty

Field:
Black Eyed Susan
Coneflower
Queen Anne's Lace
Yarrow
Butterfly weed
*Daylilies
Joe Pye Weed

Wetland:
Cardinal Flower
Iris

Perennials flowers:
*Daylilies
Iris
Yarrow
Columbine
*Peony
*Hosta
*Astilbe

*non-native

DECEMBER 4 1989   © 1989   THE ABOVE FORMAT AND TECHNOLOGY ARE THE PROPERTY OF ANDRES DUANY AND ELIZABETH PLATER-ZYBERK, ARCHITECTS. NO PART THEREOF SHALL BE COPIED, DISCLOSED TO OTHERS, OR USED WITHOUT THE WRITTEN CONSENT OF THE ARCHITECTS.   EIGHTH OF EIGHT SHEETS

14

12

Landscape drawings for Haymount by Warren Byrd. A plan and section showing transition from a square to a park to natural conditions.

13

A drawing of the native plant species recommended by the Code for use at Haymount.

14

The Code of recommended plants includes rules for their use on public and private land.

WELLINGTON

Palm Beach County, Florida

1

Freedom is not constituted primarily of privileges but of responsibilities.

Albert Camus

Multiple neighborhoods by various designers

Wellington is a new town of ten neighborhoods. As in much of Florida, extensive water-ways are required for drainage. At Wellington, a lake serves as the focus for the assemblage of the neighborhoods, and canals serve as surrogate greenbelts separating them.

A master plan, the TND Ordinance, and a series of shared technical requirements unify the neighborhoods, each of which was designed by a different author.

The flight path of an adjacent airport produced the geometric distortion of the master plan, which was further manipulated to terminate important street vistas with the sites of three elementary schools and a public park.

The central lake is lined by a continuous boulevard which links the commercial buildings of each neighborhood. A secondary inland boulevard connects the civic squares of each neighborhood, providing a simple bus route, which is within a five-minute walk of all residents.

Although the neighborhoods are characterized differently by distinct canal and street arrangements, each one has a full range of uses. Workplace, shopping, and apartments are adjacent to the lakefront boulevard. Other residential types grade from town-houses near the lake to larger detached homes at the opposite edge. The civic square at the center of each neighborhood has a child care facility, a corner grocery store and a meeting hall. One neighborhood is specialized to receive a university campus with a related research and development campus.

Wellington's building types, as coded by the urban and architectural regulations, represent a virtual catalog of current suburban types, adapted to behave in an urbanisti-cally responsible manner, especially in the disposition of parking.

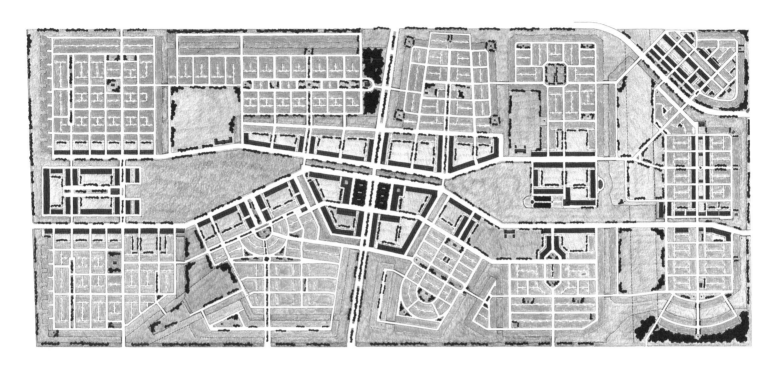

2

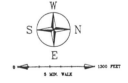

Corepoint Corporation

1,500 acres

4,400 dwelling units

1.7. million sf commercial/office

300,000 sf science and technology park

10 meeting halls

Police station

Fire station

College campus

Middle school

2 elementary schools

10 child care facilities

Designed September 1989

Permits pending

1

The site in Palm Beach County, Florida.

2

The plan for Wellington.

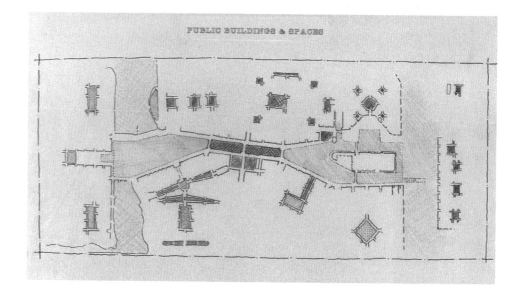

3

A diagram of public buildings and their associated spaces distributed throughout the plan. Churches and schools service the entire town; each neighborhood has its own meeting hall, child care facility, and corner store.

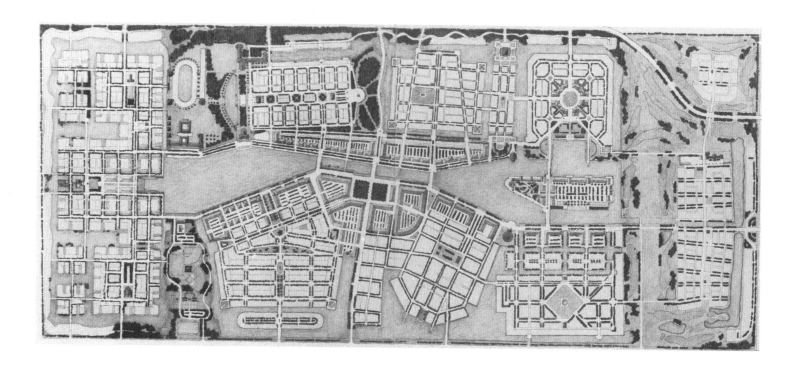

4

The charrette site plan with the different designers' neighborhoods combined for the first time before their rationalization.

5

5

A charrette drawing showing a public waterway within a residential area.

6, 7, 8

The regulations for the town of Wellington are the most recent and most sophisticated codes in this publication. They incorporate exhaustive investigation of the principal building types applied to suburban development at the time. The code respects market-derived prerogatives, but they are disciplined to define public space.

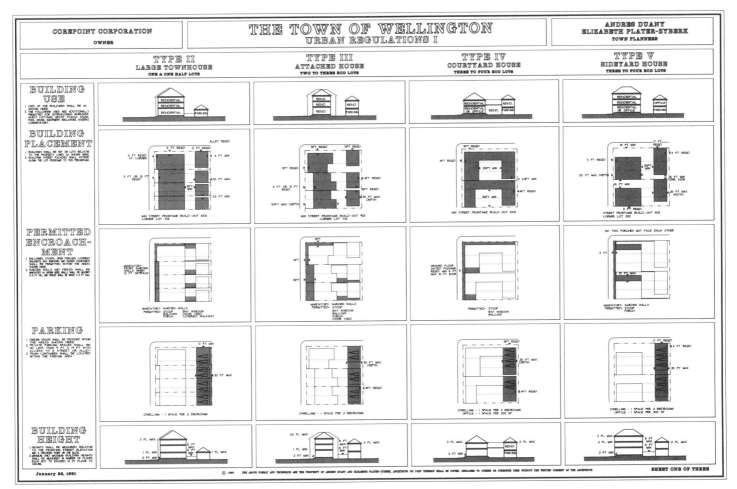

6

9

9

An aerial drawing of one of the neighborhoods shows the shops and workplaces along the main lakefront boulevard, as well as the gradation of housing types from most dense at the lakefront to least dense at the opposite edge.

10

This neighborhood incorporates a university campus seamlessly into its fabric.

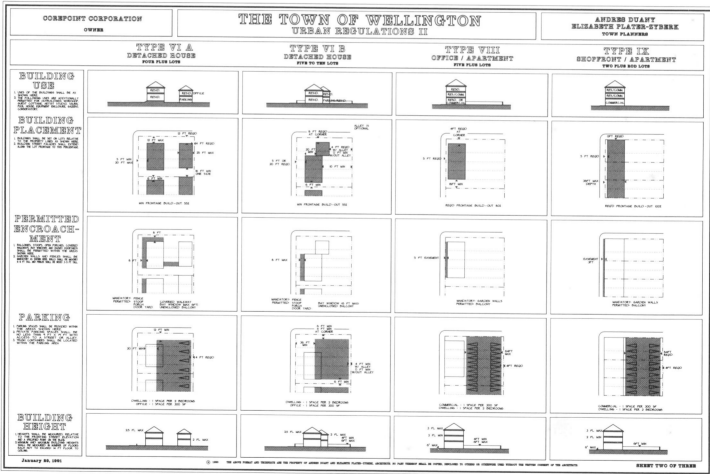

7

10

11

A drawing of a waterway on the edge of a neighborhood.

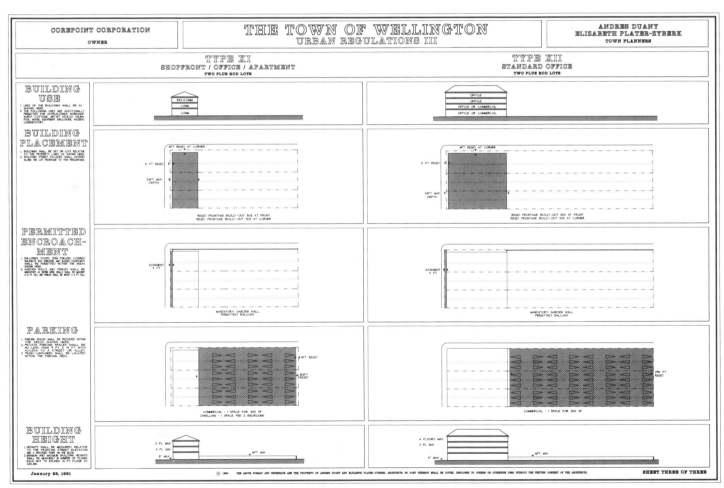

8

1

CAPITAL CITY RENAISSANCE

Trenton, New Jersey

The pseudoscience of planning seems almost neurotic in its determination to imitate empiric failure and ignore empiric success.

Jane Jacobs, 1960

An inner city redevelopment plan

This revitalization plan for the Capital District of Trenton, New Jersey, is the result of a joint venture between the Liebman-Melting Partnership and Duany and Plater-Zyberk. The plan was developed publicly in two sequential design charrettes which reviewed the city's history, the needs of its citizens, and the possibilities for its future growth.

The plan proposes several major interventions. It reconstructs a street network in areas demolished for parking during the 1960s. It creates a continuous sidewalk-based pedestrian network with primary retail streets and secondary service streets. It limits building volume to distribute density and land value equitably and predictably. And it reclaims the Delaware River embankment as an integral part of the city's public realm, replacing the unnecessary expressway with a drive and riverfront park.

Relevant pre-existing proposals by different local groups were incorporated in the plan: canal and creek-front improvements and the re-opening of the pedestrian mall to vehicular use. Existing plans for additions to the State Capitol are to be revised to include structured parking that will support the restoration of the riverfront park.

A one-page code regulates urban space and building type by prescribing height, setbacks, and ground floor use, as well as basic architectural standards such as the proportioning of wall surfaces. The plan and code are guiding new building in the Capital District today.

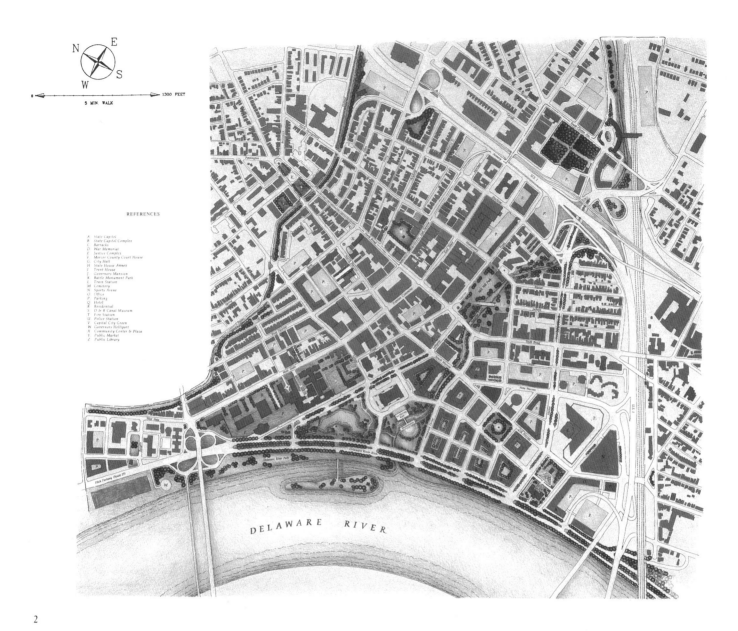

REFERENCES

A   State Capitol
B   State Capitol Complex
C   Barracks
D   War Memorial
E   Justice Complex
F   Mercer County Court House
G   City Hall
H   State House Annex
I   Trent House
J   Governors Mansion
K   Battle Monument Park
L   Train Station
M   Cemetery
N   Sports Arena
O   Office
P   Parking
Q   Hotel
R   Residential
S   D & R Canal Museum
T   Fire Station
U   Police Station
V   Capital City Green
W   Governors Heliport
X   Community Center & Plaza
Y   Public Market
Z   Public Library

DELAWARE   RIVER

2

Capital City Redevelopment Corporation
Bob Litke, Director

640 acres
Housing
Offices and shops
Civic arena
Hotel and conference center
Outdoor amphitheater and skating rink

Designed January 1989
Under construction

1
Trenton, New Jersey. The Capital District fronts the river.

2
The Capital City Renaissance Plan, showing the reestablished street grid and a new drive that, by replacing an old expressway, reclaims the riverfront for public use.

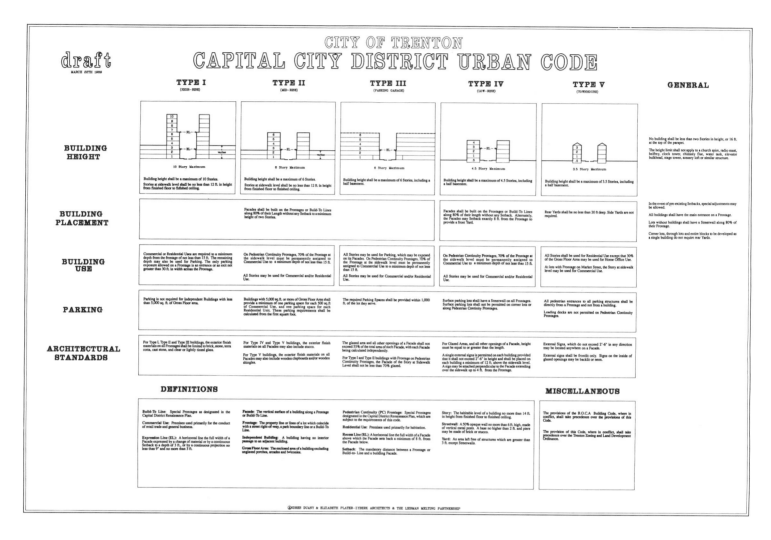

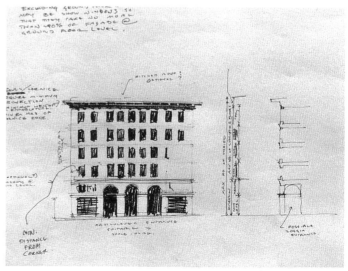

3

The Capital City District Urban Code, enacted in 1989.

4

A charrette study of building heights and setbacks.

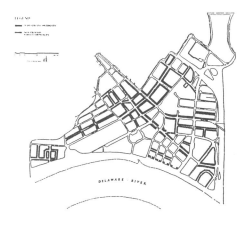

5

A drawing of the existing street network showing large areas of discontinuity.

6

A drawing showing the reestablishment of the street network.

7

A drawing indicating streets that are critical to a continuous pedestrian network. Buildings along these streets are required to have at street level a minimum of 70 percent shopfront usage and 70 percent minimum of glazing.

8

The existing conditions show the Delaware River dominated by a highway, precluding public use of the waterfront.

9

A charrette drawing of the proposed drive, replacing the expressway along the river. The drive is lined with apartment buildings developed on land whose increased value will defray the cost of roadway demolition and reconstruction.

9

MASHPEE COMMONS

Mashpee, Massachussetts

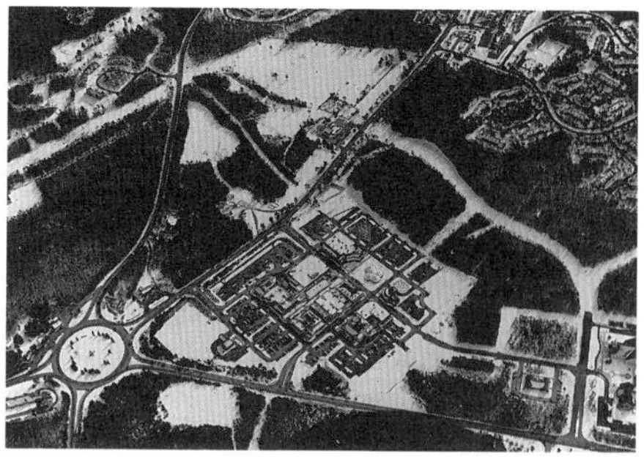

1

*The artificial separation of houses and work creates intolerable rifts in peoples'
inner lives.*

Christopher Alexander, 1977

The restructuring of a strip shopping center

The plan for Mashpee Commons expands the owner's initiative to convert an existing
strip shopping center into a town center. A plan by the Cavendish Partnership cut a
grid of new streets through the existing buildings and added new buildings, with
shops below and other uses above, to create an alternative urbanism to the highway.
The new streets, Market and Main, became the basis for subsequent planning. Market
Street was extended in one direction to a new town green, incorporating a church, a
library, and a meeting hall.

The Duany and Plater-Zyberk plan expands the town's area and activities. Market
Street is extended east across an existing highway to connect the town center to a new
neighborhood. Main Street connects north to another commercial center. Along these
trajectories, the streets are lined continuously with stores and sidewalk pergolas to screen
the parking lots and to create spatial continuity for pedestrians. Several compact residential neighborhoods beyond natural preserves complete the plan. Each has a green and a
site for a civic building.

The plan and codes present several strategies for responding to Cape Cod's shortage
of affordable housing: requiring apartments above shops, placing apartments and townhouses within walking distance of the center, allowing streets to mix housing types, and
encouraging outbuilding rental units ("granny flats") on single family lots.

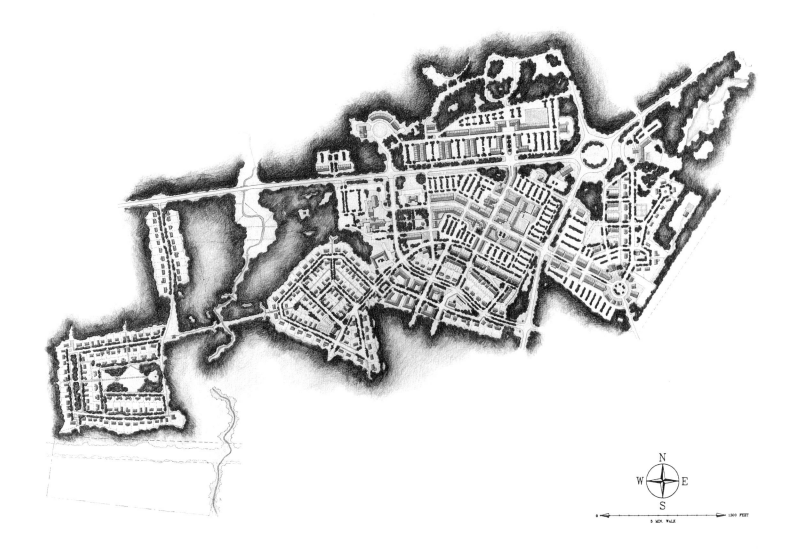

2

Fields Point Limited Partnership, owner
Arnold B. Chace, Jr., developer

Designed August 1988
Under construction

278 acres
300 dwelling units
718,000 sf commercial/office
Senior housing
75-room hotel
Town hall
2 places of worship
Post office
Library
Fire station
Police station
Child care facility

1
An aerial view of Mashpee Commons: The 1960s shopping center under conversion into a town center. The old parking lots remain; the village streets are new.

2
The master plan for Mashpee Commons. The old shopping center is southwest of the rotary.

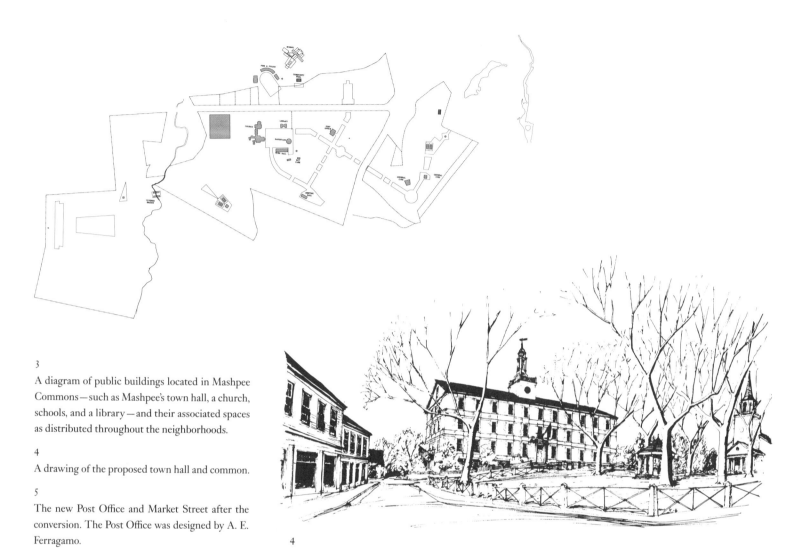

3

A diagram of public buildings located in Mashpee Commons—such as Mashpee's town hall, a church, schools, and a library—and their associated spaces as distributed throughout the neighborhoods.

4

A drawing of the proposed town hall and common.

5

The new Post Office and Market Street after the conversion. The Post Office was designed by A. E. Ferragamo.

6

The Sentry Federal Building is designed by Ellenzweig Associates; the Steeple Street Building (foreground) is by Prellwitz/Chilinski Architects.

4

5

6

TERRITORIES

*The thought must arise even in circles untouched by Art, that without . . .
largeness of conception and breadth of vision . . . and without the constant hand
and touch of Art upon every detail, a beautiful city can never be built.*

Otto Wagner, 1912

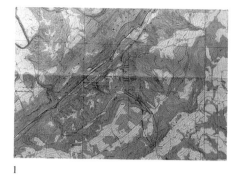

1

BLOUNT SPRINGS

Blount Springs, Alabama

*Theories of formalism and informalism have been allowed to develop into preju-
dices held without real appreciation of the true relationship of formality of design
and informality of site.*

Raymond Unwin, 1911

A town and several villages in a wooded, hilly landscape

Blount Springs, Alabama, was originally founded in the nineteenth century. Mineral
springs and water courses in steep forest terrain attracted and supported a flourishing
population until 1915, when much of the town burned.

The master plan for a new Blount Springs seeks to re-create a community in
harmony with its history and its environment. The Town, a focus for surrounding villages,
is located on a hill overlooking a new lake. The crest of the hill is given to a square, from
which streets emanate to the lakefront, to the railroad station, and to adjacent villages.
The ruins of the original settlement are to remain within a park to the west of the Town
Center.

Each village has public spaces and buildings and sometimes modest commercial
offerings. Blue Hole Village, the first under construction, is organized around a new lake.
Each of its neighborhoods is centered on a green or park exhibiting a unique natural
feature to give the neighborhood particular character: Crescent Green is the only formal,
lawned space; the Hollow is a large sink hole with specimen trees; Ridge Road's long axis
is bisected by a square with a monument.

A power line cut through the forest is maintained to display the rolling landscape,
crossing several high points marked with pavilions and monuments.

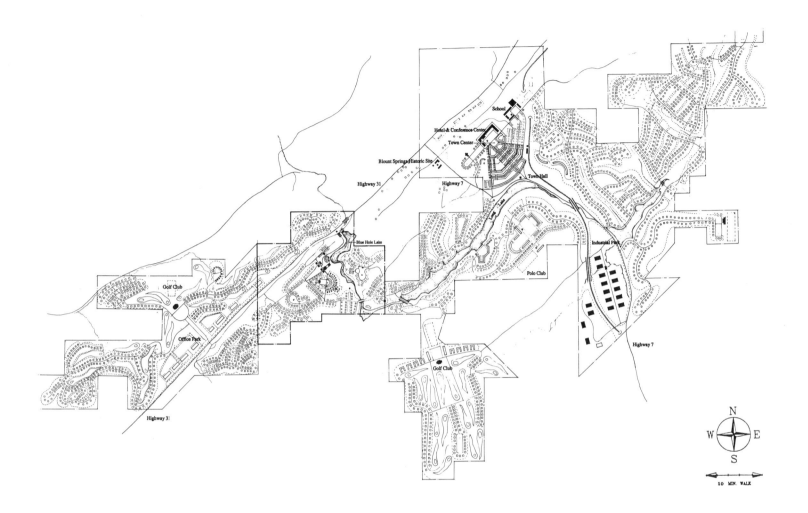

2

Drennen Land and Timber Co., Ltd.
5000 acres, The Town of Blount Springs

Blount Springs Recolonization Partners, Ltd.
450 acres, Blue Hole Village

110 dwelling units
10,000 sf commercial/office
Meeting hall
Inn
Outdoor amphitheater
Child care facility

Designed January 1988
Blue Hole Village under construction

1
A USGS map of Blount Springs showing the steep topography.

2
The plan for Blount Springs.

3

An early plan for the Blount Springs Town Center,
the second phase of development.

4

A drawing of Blue Hole Village, the first phase of
development.

5

Elevation analysis of the Blue Hole Village site.

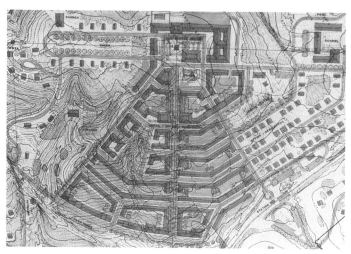

3

4

5

6

6

A drawing of the Village Green.

7

The Welcome Center as seen from the entry to Blue Hole Village along Old Highway 31.

8

The Blue Hole Lake and dam as seen from the Welcome Center.

9

A ridge house overlooking Blue Hole Lake.

7

8

9

1

N A N C E   C A N Y O N

Chico, California

A Garden City is a Town designed for healthy living and industry; of a size that makes possible a full measure of social life, but not larger; surrounded by a rural belt; the whole of the land being in public ownership or held in trust for the community.

Ebenezer Howard, 1898

A town plan with ecological attributes

Nance Canyon's nine villages are situated on a series of ridges bordering the canyon which dominates the site. The developers' ecological sensitivity was addressed in several ways: by organizing the built areas in walking-scale villages; by the optimum solar orientation of and detailing of the streets and buildings; by incorporating advanced techniques for water conservation and waste water treatment; and by preserving most of the site.

The new community's economy will be based on a substantial research and development industry related to California State University at Chico. The university will open a branch campus in one of the villages.

The typical village design is linear, respecting the topography and tree groupings. Each village is organized by a pair of one-way main streets separated by a series of public buildings and greens, a pattern loosely derived from that of the town of Chico. This linear civic center is lined by commercial and residential buildings. It can remain undeveloped, functioning as a green, until the demand for public buildings spurs its development.

Streets are designed so that buildings provide shade. Specific overlay codes control architectural expression according to solar orientation. Trees, which grow with difficulty in this area, typically are reserved for the larger public spaces; along neighborhood streets, they are placed in private yards, their canopies extending into the street space.

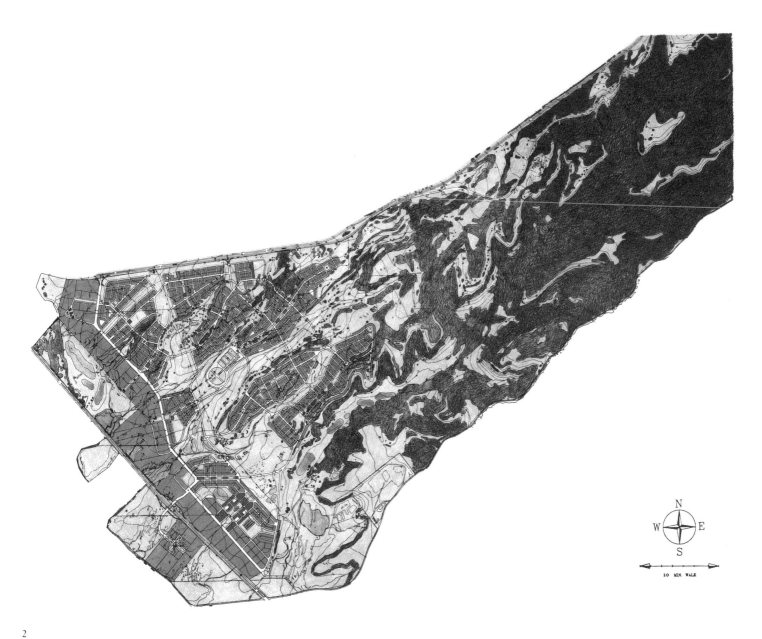

2

Blakeley Swartz, owner
Tom DiGiovanni, developer
Steve Honeycutt, developer

3,050 acres
5,000 dwelling units
800,000 sf industrial
700,000 sf commercial/office
Hospital and medical center
Town hall
Post office
Library
Fire station

Police station
College campus extension
High school
Middle school
2 elementary schools
9 sites for child care facilities
Regional park

Designed May 1990
Permits pending

1

An aerial photograph of the site shows the tree groupings along the escarpments of the canyon.

2

The plan of Nance Canyon shows nine villages grouped toward the highway, leaving two thirds of the site, including the canyon, undeveloped and available for recreation.

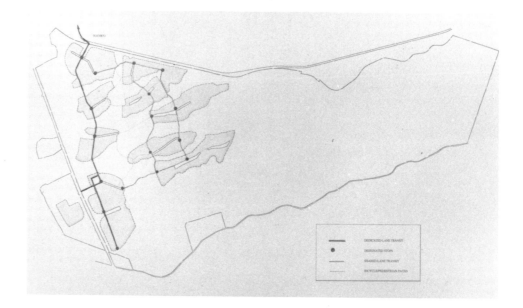

3

The villages straddle ridges and are separated by greenbelts. A bus system will link the villages, with stops at each village green.

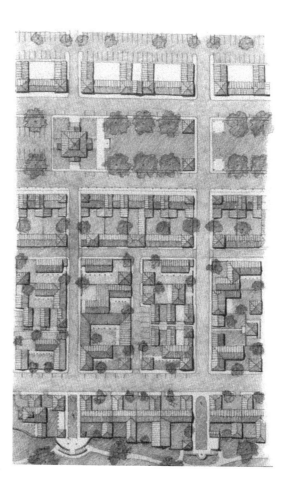

4

A detail of a village shows the public green flanked by two main streets; the commercial buildings, behind which lie the residential courtyard buildings; and the large houses at the edge. Public buildings, businesses, services, and housing of different types are closely grouped.

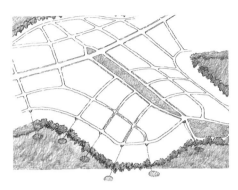

5

Village greens are shaped by twin one-way main streets which run along the ridges.

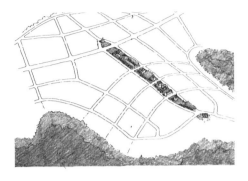

6

The long greens are the location for public buildings. As buildings are added according to need, the green will become a series of squares.

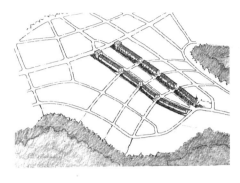

7

Buildings lining the pair of main streets have shops on the first floor and offices or apartments on the second floor.

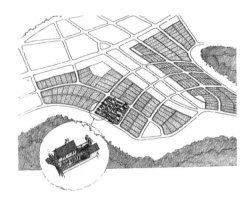

8

The residential areas adjacent to the village center are typically developed with courtyard buildings on relatively small lots.

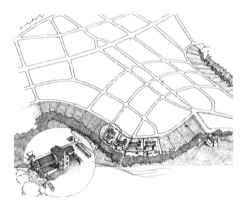

9

The edges of the villages are almost rural in character, with detached houses on large lots.

10

Workplaces are located at the edge of the village.

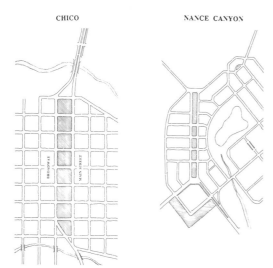

CHICO   NANCE CANYON

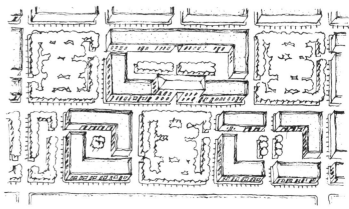

Work Place and Parking Gardens

12

11

The one-way main streets of Nance Canyon are modeled on those of Chico. Through the central park and public buildings, this device turns Main Street into a civic as well a commercial center. In addition, the splitting of traffic eases pedestrian crossing.

12

A charrette sketch of workplaces and parking lots.

13

A charrette sketch showing the green subdivided to host public buildings.

14

View of a village as seen from across the greenbelt.

15

Andres Duany and Gerald Blakely, co-founder of Nance Canyon, discussing the project during the charrette.

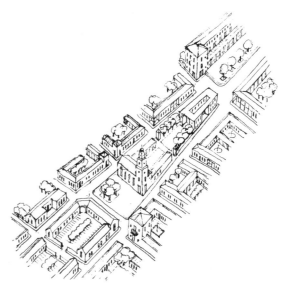

Town Center

13

14

15

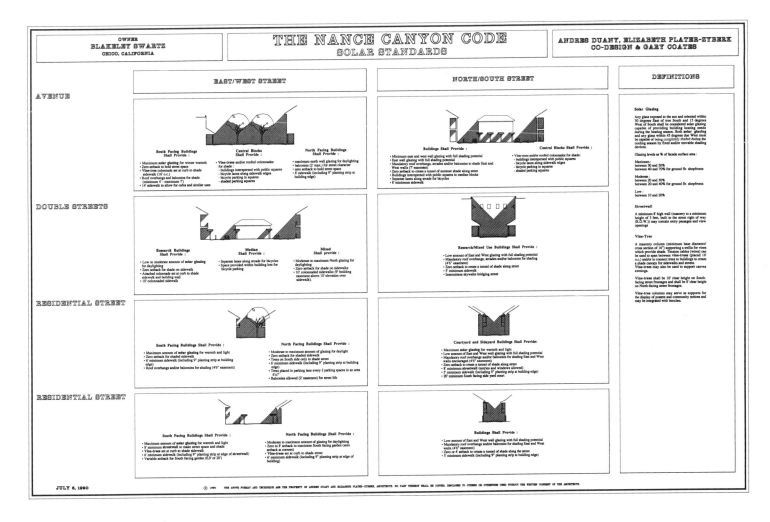

16
The Solar Code employs architectural elements to shade the streets and the buildings. Local conditions demanded this overlay code, which keys urban design to orientation.

17
View of an east-west street. Buildings on the south side shade the street.

18
View of a north-south street. Overhanging balconies shade the street.

17

18

1

AVALON PARK

Orlando, Florida

I am a mother of four children who are not able to leave the yard because of our city's design. Ever since we moved here I have felt like a caged animal only let out for a ride in the car. It is impossible to walk even to the grocery store two blocks away.

A mother in Tulsa, Oklahoma writing to
Andres Duany, July 18, 1990

A regional plan

Avalon Park is a design of regional scale. Four towns and six villages are organized on the mile-square Jeffersonian grid that is distorted by the Econlockhatchee River and its adjacent wetlands. More than half the site is reserved for the river estuaries, wetlands, and retention ponds which are incorporated into greenbelts between the towns and villages; smaller wetlands and hammocks are incorporated within neighborhood parks.

Villages and towns are composed of three or four neighborhoods. Each neighborhood is planned with the radius of a five-minute walk and each one provides basic neighborhood services such as a child care facility, a general store, and a meeting hall. Each village has a limited number of shops and workplace. The towns have a larger commercial component because they are located at the intersections of the major roads. They are specialized according to the regional services they provide.

One of the towns contains a university campus and sites for important cultural institutions around a circular lake. Another features a large component of first-class office space with its attendant services. These office buildings surround a bosque that serves as overflow parking and assists in the reduction of the required parking load.

The two other towns include retail centers. One combines the programmatic and marketing requirements of a regional mall with that of a downtown main street: the extensive parking and department stores are conventionally visible from the expressway; at the same time, the department stores face a main street which conceals the parking behind a line of office and apartment buildings. The fourth town contains the retail space normally associated with a strip shopping center. While fulfilling the commercial requirements of this type, it is restructured to focus on a green, rather than on its parking lots. All four town centers have seamless street connections to the adjacent neighborhoods.

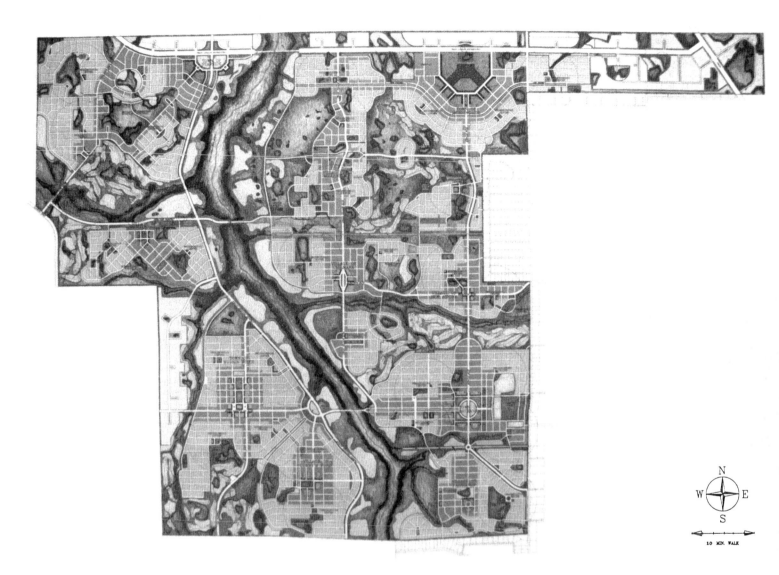

2

Flag Development Company, Inc.

9,400 acres
25,000 dwelling units
14 million sf office
3.3 million sf commercial
1,900 hotel rooms
850 nursing home beds
500 congregate care beds
Hospital, 4 clinics
10 meeting halls
10 places of worship

4 libraries
Junior college
15 schools
30 child care facilities

Designed December 1989
Permits pending

1
An aerial photograph of the site east of Orlando with the Econlockhatchee River bisecting it.

2
The master plan for Avalon Park.

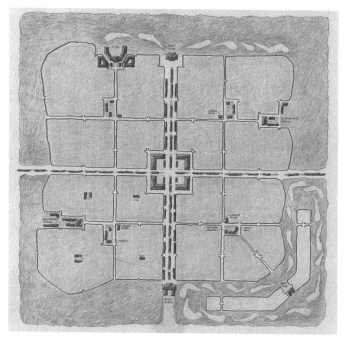

3

The schematic regional plan before the specific design of each town and village.

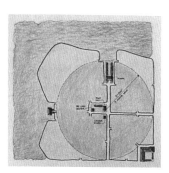
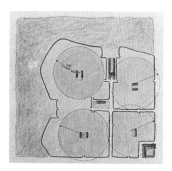

4

Each neighborhood is sized so that the majority of the dwellings are within five-minutes walking distance of the neighborhood square where the meeting hall, a child care facility, a corner store and the bus stop are located.

5

Each neighborhood also has playgrounds within two-minutes walking distance of most dwellings.

6

An aggregation of neighborhoods forms a village or a town, with a large retail component centered among them, straddling the principal traffic routes.

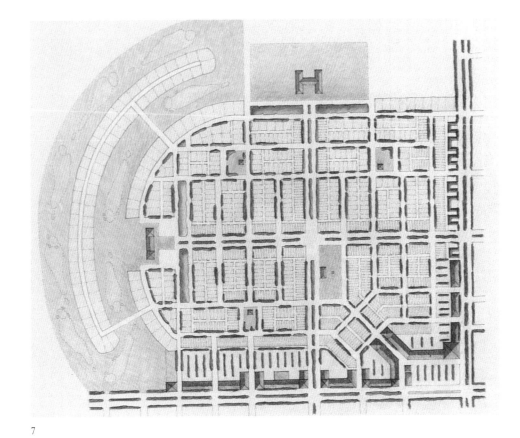

7

7
A drawing of a hypothetical neighborhood showing a portion of the shopping and workplace along boulevards on two edges, and the school and golf club sharing the greenbelt on the other two edges for their facilities.

8
A drawing of a neighborhood center showing its essential elements: corner store, bus stop, and meeting hall.

9
A drawing of a neighborhood playground and child care facility.

8

10
The planning team walked parts of the site.

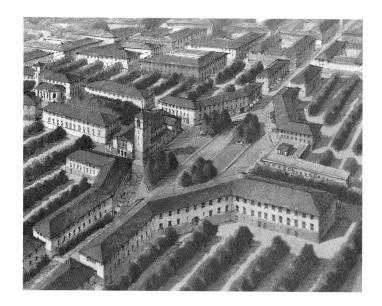

11

Plans for village centers.

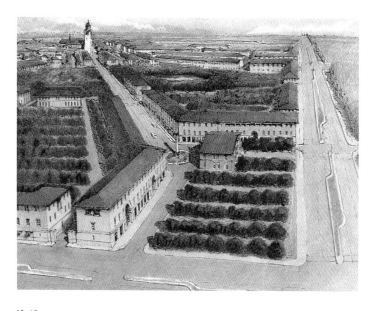

12, 13

Aerial views of village centers.

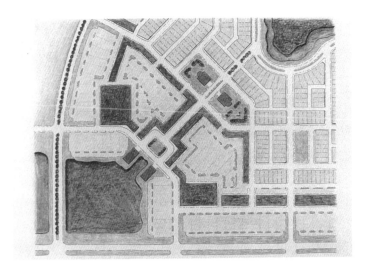

14
A plan for a town center incorporating a strip convenience center.

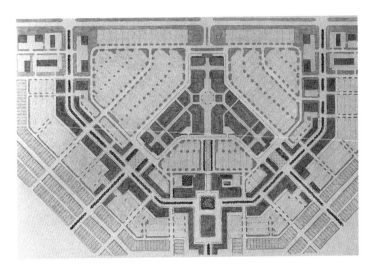

15
A plan for a town center incorporating a regional
mall.

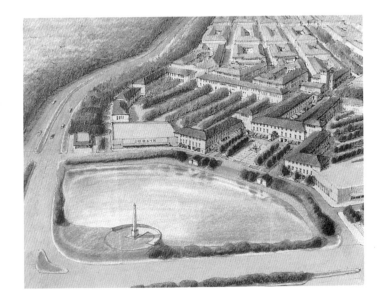

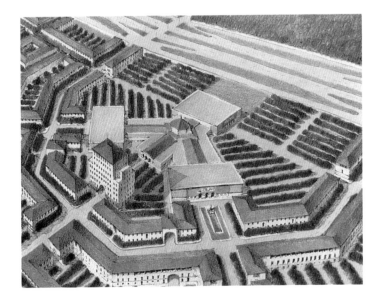

16, 17
Aerial views of town centers.

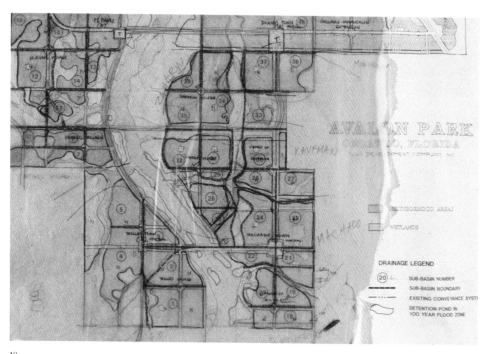

18

An early charrette diagram of the towns and villages and their assignments to designers.

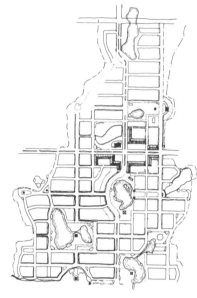

19

A village design by Kamal Zaharin.

20

A town design by Elizabeth Plater-Zyberk and Jean-François LeJeune.

21

A town and a village design by Jorge and Luis Trelles.

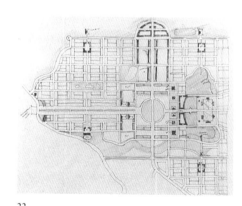

22

A town design by Rodolfo Machado and Carlos Aparicio.

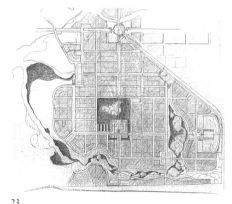

23

A village design by Charles Barrett.

CODES

For a city to be well built, the exterior of buildings cannot be left to the wishes of private citizens. Everything in a street must be approved by public authorities and abide by general rules established for the design of streets. It is necessary to establish by law the sites on which buildings can be erected, but also the manner in which this should be done.

Laugier, *Essai sur l'Architecture*

The Codes

William Lennertz

Regulatory codes lie at the heart of Duany and Plater-Zyberk's work. Early in their work they realized that existing zoning ordinances—more than economics or planning and design philosophies—were impediments to achieving more urbane communities. Conventional zoning frequently works to segregate activities. Duany and Plater-Zyberk set out to reform zoning to do the opposite—to connect, to aggregate, and to unify. The evolution of these codes—from the earliest regulations written for Seaside to the documents developed for more recent projects—is illustrated on the following pages.

The codes, as they have come to be standardized, consist of five documents: 1) Regulating Plan, 2) Urban Regulations, 3) Architectural Regulations, 4) Street Sections, and 5) Landscape Regulations. Occasionally a summary of standard building types and a plan for a composite block are included to illustrate the Urban Regulations.

Duany and Plater-Zyberk have also developed codes that may be introduced within the complexities of existing communities. Trenton's urban code, for example, addresses the architectural and urban issues of a dense downtown. And the Traditional Neighborhood Development Ordinance is a comprehensive code for municipalities whose existing bylaws preclude the creation of traditional neighborhoods.

The Regulating Plan. This drawing fixes, with technical precision, the information which is more loosely rendered in the Master Plan. It identifies the street types which are shown in the Street Sections, and shows the public tracts reserved for squares, parks, and civic buildings. It also shows the platting of the private building lots and assigns their corresponding building types.

The Urban Regulations. This matrix regulates those aspects of the private building types which pertain to and help form the public realm. It is different from conventional zoning codes not only in format, but also in that, rather than being generally proscriptive, it is specifically prescriptive. For example, all buildings must place a specified percentage of their street facades on a common frontage line, and parking is relegated to the rear of the lots to avoid discontinuities in the street frontage. Social issues are addressed also: for example, outbuildings with rental apartments on single family lots are encouraged, to provide a range of ages and income levels in all housing districts. The Urban Regulations encourage the provision of certain building elements which influence social behavior such as stoops, porches and garden walls.

The Architectural Regulations. This matrix regulates configurations, materials, and techniques of construction. The configuration controls are intended to produce harmony among buildings. The control of materials and methods encourages new buildings to relate to the history, geography and climate of the place. Because urban quality can be enhanced by architectural coherence, but is not necessarily dependent on it, the Architectural Regulations range from the strictly deterministic, as in Windsor, to the liberal, as in Avalon.

Only private buildings are subject to the provisions of the Urban and Architectural Regulations, since private buildings are the material used to define public spaces. Public buildings, on the other hand, are monuments, intended to be differentiated from this basic material.

The Street Types. This drawing depicts the character of the public spaces. The intention is to make places where pedestrians feel safe and comfortable, as well as to provide for adequate automobile movement. The proportion of building height to street width is clearly specified, together with the width of travel and parking lanes, the alignment of trees, and the sidewalk width. The variations are related to the intended urban or rural character of the street as much as to utilitarian concerns. A full range of streets may include highways, avenues, and boulevards to carry regional traffic, streets for high density residential and commercial traffic, roads and lanes for low density residential areas, and service alleys.

The Landscape Regulations. These specify the planting for streets, squares and parks to support the character of each place. With few exceptions, native species are preferred, and planting on private lots is limited to species selected for drought-tolerance and suitability as habitats for local fauna. The choices are limited, and directed toward the goal of achieving a naturalistic reforestation of the town.

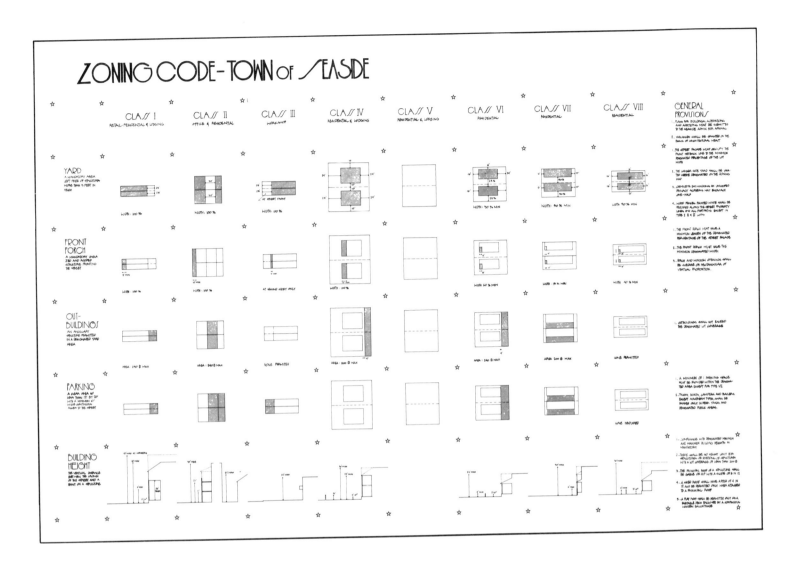

ZONING CODE – TOWN OF SEASIDE

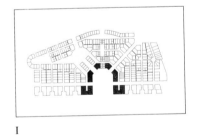

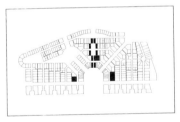
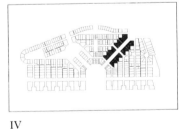

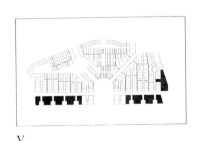

I

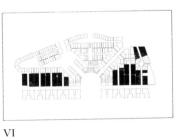

II

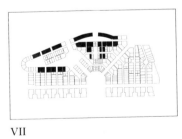

III

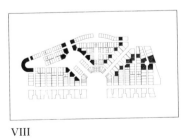

IV

V

VI

VII

VIII

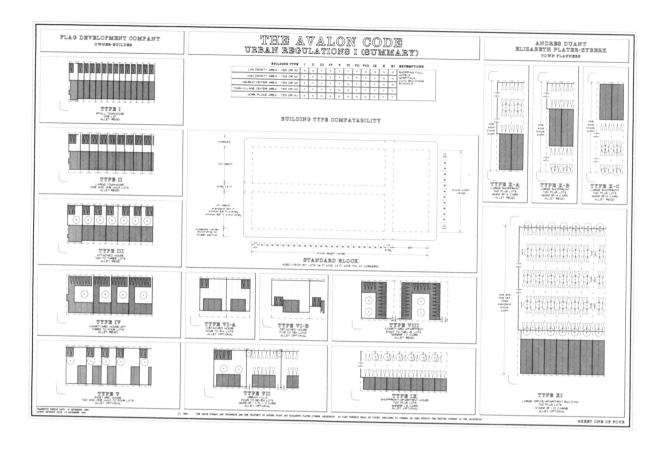

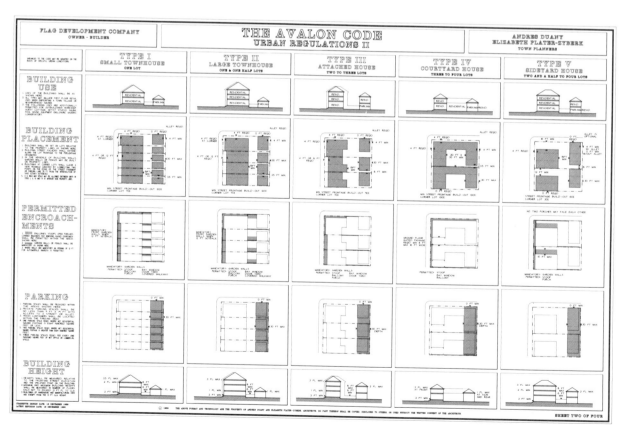

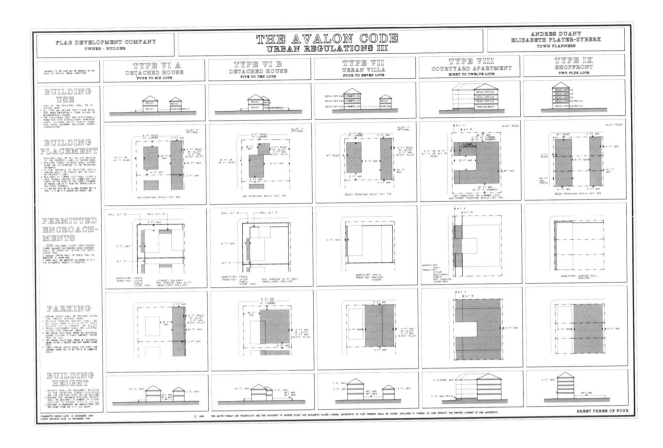

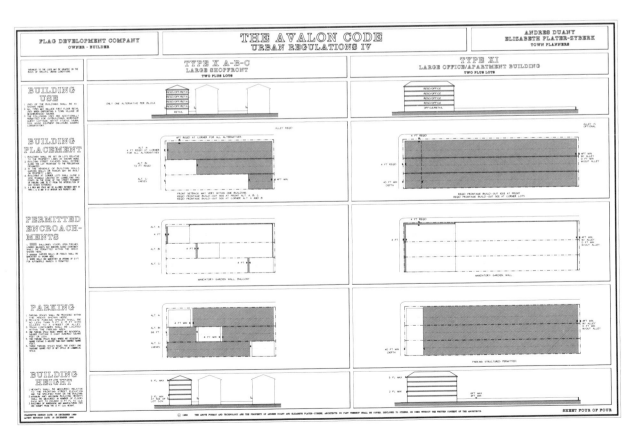

FLAG
DEVELOPMENT COMPANY

THE AVALON CODE
ARCHITECTURAL REGULATIONS

ANDRES DUANY
ELIZABETH PLATER-ZYBERK
TOWN PLANNERS

	BUILDING WALLS	BUILDING ELEMENTS	ROOFS	WINDOWS & DOORS	GARDEN WALLS
MATERIALS	Building walls may be clad in wood clapboard, wood dropsiding, wood board and batten or Wolverine premium vinyl siding. Building walls may be finished in brick selected from the Town Architect's List. Building walls may be finished in smooth stucco. Building walls may be made of split-faced block, pre-cast concrete or cast stone.	Columns, posts, balconies, porches and bay windows shall be made of wood. Columns, piers and arches may be made of brick or stucco. Stoops may be made of brick, stucco , cast concrete or pressure treated wood. Fences and railings may be made of steel or aluminium sections. Signs shall be made of canvas or wood.	Roofs may be clad with red cedar shingles, terra cotta tile, concrete tile or galvanized steel. Gutters shall be made of galvanized steel, copper, or painted aluminum.	Windows and doors shall be made of aluminum, wood or vinyl-clad wood. Windows and doors shall be glazed in clear glass with no more than a 10% daylight reduction.	Garden walls may be finished in brick, stucco or concrete block matching the principal building. Fences shall be made of wood pickets, lattice or boards.
CONFIGURATION	Two or more wall materials may be combined on one facade only horizontally. Exterior chimneys shall be finished in brick or stucco. Cantilevers, except as open balconies, are not permitted.	Columns, if provided, shall be of the Tuscan or Doric orders with proportions and moldings according to The American Vignola. Spindles and balusters on balconies, porches and decks shall not exceed 5" on center. Porch and loggia openings shall be square or vertical in proportion. Balconies shall not exceed 3' in depth. Bay windows shall be habitable spaces carried to the ground. Steel railings shall not exceed 4" on center. Signs may be no bigger than 36" in vertical dimension.	Principal building roofs shall be symmetrical gables or hips, pitched between 4:12 and 8:12. Shed (monopitch) roofs shall be attached to the highest point of the the principal building. The pitch of a shed roof shall be no less than 2:12. Flat roofs shall be enclosed by parapets no less than 42" high. Dormers shall be placed a minimum of 36" from side building walls. Dormers shall be roofed with a symmetrical gable or hip. Gutters shall be half-round at overhanging eaves and ogee at tight eaves.	Windows may be square or vertical in proportion. Additionally, windows may be circular or hexagonal. Garage doors shall be a maximum width of 9'. The following are permitted accessories: - wood shutters sized to match openings - canvas awnings (except circular geometries)	Brick or stucco walls shall be no less than 8" wide and capped. Fences shall be made with no more than 3" gaps between pickets. Fences and walls at street fronts shall be between 36" and 54" in height. The undercroft of decks shall be enclosed by wood lattice.
TECHNIQUE	Clapboard shall be 3.5" to 6" to the weather. Dropsiding shall not exceed 10" to the weather. Board and batten shall not exceed 10" and 2" running alternately. Board trim at corners and around openings shall not exceed 4" to the weather except at the front door surround which may be any size or configuration. Board trim shall be flush with the wall surface. Brick shall be laid in a true bonding pattern (no stack or running "bond"). Brick mortar joints shall be struck and no more than 1/2" wide. Stucco shall be smooth sand finish. Concrete block shall be split-faced precast concrete	Brick and stucco arches shall be no less than 12" in depth. Piers shall be no less than 12" x 12 " Wood posts shall be no less than 5" x 5" and chamfered at the corners. Canvas signs may be internally lit. Wood signs may be externally lit.	Overhanging eaves shall expose rafters. Taught eaves shall be finished by a molding.	Rectangular windows shall be hinged casement, single or double hung. Dormer windows may be hinged casement or hopper. Circular and hexagonal windows may be fixed or pivot. All doors must be hinged except garage doors. Sliding doors are permitted at backyard locations only The total glazing area on the facade shall not exceed 30% of the facade surface.	Wood fences shall be painted white.

DECEMBER 18, 1989

FLAG
DEVELOPMENT COMPANY

THE AVALON CODE
LANDSCAPE REGULATIONS

CANIN ASSOCIATES
LANDSCAPE ARCHITECTS

PROCEDURES

PLANTING OF PUBLIC TRACTS

All trees in public tracts shall be nursery grown, ball and burlapped. No collected material will be accepted. All trees shall have a minimum of 2-1/2" to 3" caliper with a 14' to 16' height. These trees shall limb up (clear trunk) a minimum 4-1/2" to 5" cal. with a 18' to 20' height. These trees shall limb up a minimum of 8' above ground line. One tree type shall be selected per trafficway (avenue, boulevard,etc....)

PLANTING OF PRIVATE LOTS

A. Existing trees of all caliper shall be encouraged to remain where use and grading requirements allow. This will form clusters of tree species with old, large caliper trees and smaller seedlings; small native habitats/niche conserved.

B. There shall be at least one tree of the species listed below (of not less than 3-1/2" caliper) planted in a front or rear yard for each 16' of street frontage.

C. The use of native species of trees, shrubs, vines, groundcovers and perrenials is encouraged in order to make gardens compatible with the existing wildlife habitat and its regional context.

D. The use of fruit, berry and nut trees is encouraged in order to contribute to the existing wildlife habitat.

E. Planting of fruit trees in groups of four or greater (regularly spaced) is encouraged to create small orchards.

F. Planting of nut trees in regular or irregularly-spaced groups of three or more is encouraged.

G. All shrubs should be planted in groups of at least ten (of like species) rather than as individuals. (Minimum spacing : 2 feet on center for hedges.up to 5 feet on center maximum for open plantings).

H. Plantings in immediate proximity to buildings should respect architectural lines (that is, should be seen as extensions of the architectural walls), whereas plantings towards the backs of yards could take on more irregular and "naturalized" configurations and spacings.

I. Plantings toward the street should respect the integrity of the street. Plantings should not obscure the buildings and should respect views to and from streets, porches, walks and public parks.

FERTILIZER MANAGEMENT

Soil tests of areas to be fertilized will be conducted anually to determine adequate nutrient requirements and prevent over-fertilization of nitrogen, phosphorus and potassium. Fertilization will not exceed specified rates.

PESTICIDE MANAGEMENT

Town Environmental manager will prepare an integrated pest management (IPM) plan for the major species of concern, and guide its implementation. Such plan will aim to reduce amounts of chemical applications.

Pesticides will be applied only in accordance with label instruction. No pesticides will be allowed to contact water surface. Acceptable filter strip widths will be prescribed by the environmental manager.

A pesticide disposal plan will be prepared and implemented by the environmental manager. Pesticide containers and unused pesticide will be disposed of in accordance with the plan.

PLANTING ON PUBLIC TRACTS

LARGE SQUARE & PARK	Primary trees should be: Quercus virginiana (Live Oak) 2-1/2"-3" cal.min. Trees on the grounds of civic bldg's. Include/consider: Liquidambar styraciflua (Sweet Gum) Magnolia grandiflora (Southern Magnolia) Ulmus parviflora (Drake Elm) Washingtonia robusta (Mexican Fan Palm) Phoenix Canariensis (Canary Island Date Palm) In Parks also include /consider: Acer rubrum (Red Maple) Magnolia virginiana (Sweet Bay) Taxodium distichum (Bald Cypress) Pinus elliotti (Slash Pine Densa) Pinus taeda (Loblolly Pine) Pinus clausa (Sand Pine)
SMALL RESIDENTIAL SQUARE	Trees: (24' spacing on center) (Selection depends on streets) Quercus virginiana (Live Oak) Liquidambar styraciflua (Sweet Gum) Magnolia grandiflora 'Glen St. Mary' (Southern Magnolia 'Glen St. Mary') Ilex opaca (American Holly) Lagerstroemia indica (Crape Myrtle)
AVENUE	Trees: (varies 24',32', 40',48' on center) Magnolia virginiana ' 'Glen St. Mary'(Southern Magnolia 'Glen St. Mary') Liquidambar styraciflua (Sweet Gum) Ulmus parviflora (Drake Elm) Quercus virginiana (Live Oak)
BOULEVARD	(Spacing 24', 32', 40', 48' on center) Quercus virginiana (Live Oak) Quercus shumardii (Shumard Oak)
LARGE STREET	Trees: (Spacing 24' on center) Quercus virginiana (Live Oak)
SMALL STREET	Ulmus parviflora (Drake Elm)
DRIVE	Upland Trees: (Spacing 24' on center) Quercus virginiana (Live Oak) Ilex opaca (American Holly) Pinus taeda (Loblolly Pine) Juniperus silicicola (Southern Red Cedar) Wetland Trees: (Spacing 24' or 48' on center) Taxodium distichum (Bald Cypress) Acer rubrum (Red Maple) Liquidambar styraciflua (Sweet Gum) Gordonia lazianthus (Loblolly Bay)
ROADS	Trees: (Spacing variable: min.8', max. 64') Quercus virginiana (Live Oak) Taxodium distichum (Bald Cypress) Smaller Trees: Ilex opaca (American Holly) Lagerstroemia indica (Crape Myrtle) Acer rubrum (Red Maple) Ilex cassine (Dahoon)

PLANTING ON PRIVATE LOTS

DECIDUOUS CANOPY TREES	Liquidambar styraciflua (Sweet Gum) Platanus occidentalis (Sycamore) Taxodium distichum (Bald Cypress)
MEDIUM CANOPY DECIDUOUS TREES	Acer rubrum (Red Maple) Betula nigra (River Birch)
SMALL EVERGREEN UNDERSTORY TREES	Myrica cerifera (Wax Myrtle)
SMALL FLOWERING UNDERSTORY TREES	Lagerstroemia indica (Crape Myrtle) Cornus florida (Flowering Dogwood) Ilex cassine (Dahoon Holly) Magnolia virginiana (Sweet Bay) Gordonia lazianthus (Loblolly Bay) Chionanthus virginica (Fringe Tree) Feijoa sellowiana (Pineapple Guava).
FRUIT AND NUT TREES	Citrus spp (Orange, Grapefruit, Lemon, etc.) Psidium cattleianum Persea americana (Avocado) Carya glabra (Hickory Nut)
PALMS	Washingtonia robusta (Mexican Fan Palm) Sabal palmetto (Cabbage Palm) Phoenix canariensis (Canary Island Date Palm)
EVERGREEN CANOPY TREES	Quercus virginiana (Live Oak) Magnolia grandiflora (Southern Magnolia)
EVERGREEN TREES	Pinus elliotii (Slash Pine) Pinus taeda (Loblolly Pine) Pinus palustris (Longleaf Pine) Ilex opaca (American Holly) Pinus clausa (Sand Pine) Ilex cassine (Dahoon Holly) Myrica cerifera (Wax Myrtle) Juniperus silicicola (Southern Red Cedar) Gordonia lazianthus (Loblolly Bay)
EVERGREEN SHRUBS	Ilex Cornuta 'Burfordii nana (Dwarf Bufford) Pittosporum tobira 'Variegata' (Variegated Pittosporum) Juniperus Chinensis Pfitzerana 'Nick's Compacta' (Nicks Compacta) Illicium floridanum Red Anise) Rhodendron (Azalea) Eleagnus pungens (Eleagnus) Ilex glabra (Gallberry) Illicium floridanum (Red Anise) Serenoa repens (Saw Palmetto) Sabal minor (Blue Palmetto) Viburnum Obovatum (Walter's Viburnum) Ligustrum japonicum (Wax Leaf Ligustrum)
DECIDUOUS SHRUBS	Callicarpa americana (Beauty Berry) Rhododendron austrinum (Flame Azalea) Rhododendron canescens (Wild Azalea) Pyracantha coccinea (Firethorn)
VINES	Wisteria sinensis (Wisteria) Trachelospermum jasminoides (Confederate Jasmine) Ficus repens (Fig Ivy) Lonicera sempervirens (Coral Honeysuckle) Gelsemium Sempervirens (Carolina Yellow Jasmine) Hedera helix (English Ivy)
EVERGREEN GROUNDCOVERS	Zamia pumila (Coontie) Morea iriodes (White Iris) Liriope 'Evergreen Giant'(Evergreen Giant) Pittosporum tobira 'Wheeleri' (Wheeler's Dwarf) Trachelospermum jasminoides (Star Jasmine) Vaccinium myrsinites (Dwarf Blueberry) Myrica pumila (Dwarf Wax Myrtle) Crinum americanum (Crinum Lily)
FLOWERING GROUNDCOVERS	Morea iriodes (White Iris) Hemerocallis spp. (Daylily) Rhododendron spp. (Dwarf Azalea) Raphiolepsis indica (Dwarf India Hawthorne)
WILDFLOWERS & FIELDFLOWERS	Woodland: Morea iriodes (White Iris) Impatiens wallerana(Impatiens/Busy Lizzie) Lantana camara (Lantana) Tagetes erecta (Marigold) Salvia splendens (Sage) Heuchera sanguinea (Coral Bells) Lonicera sempervirens Pentas lanceolata (Egyptian Star Cluster) Wetland: Morea iriodes (White Iris) Hymenocallis crassifolia (Spider Lily) Nephrolepsis spp (Fern)
SOD	Stenotaphrum Secondatum'Floratam' (St.Augustin Floratam')

DECEMBER 18, 1989

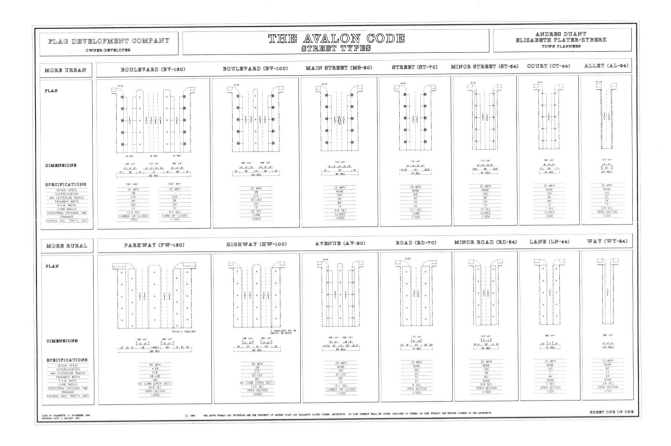

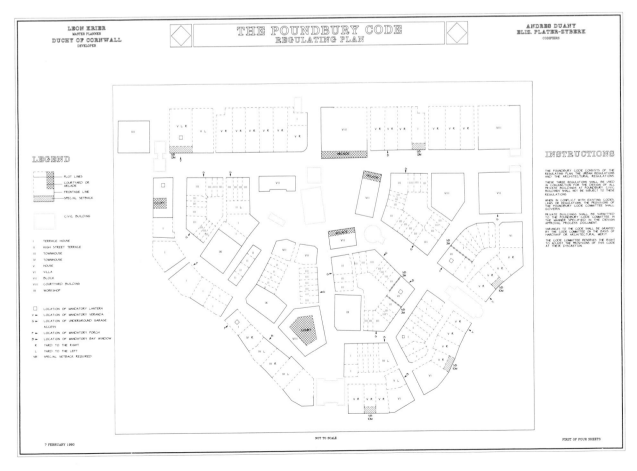

A new zoning ordinance

The congested, fragmented, unsatisfying suburbs and the disintegrating urban centers of today are not merely products of laissez-faire nor the inevitable results of mindless greed. They are thoroughly planned to be as they are: the direct result of zoning and subdivision ordinances zealously administered by planning departments.

America since World War II is largely the result of conventional subdivision and planned unit development (PUD) ordinances. If the results are dismaying, it is because the model of the city being projected is dismal. These ordinances dictate three criteria for urbanism: the free and rapid flow of traffic, parking in quantity, and the rigorous separation of uses, with the result that car traffic and social isolation have become the central, unavoidable, experience of the public realm.

The traditional pattern of walkable, mixed-use neighborhoods has been inadvertently proscribed by these ordinances. Thus, designers find themselves in the ironic situation of being forbidden from building in the manner of our admired historic places. One cannot propose a new Annapolis, Marblehead, or Key West, without seeking substantial variances from current codes.

The Traditional Neighborhood Development (TND) Ordinance restores the option of creating new development in traditional patterns by prescribing the following physical conventions.

1. The neighborhood area is limited in size, with clear edges and a focused center.
2. Shops, workplaces, schools, and residences for all income groups are located in close proximity.
3. Streets are sized and detailed to serve equitably the needs of the automobile and the pedestrian.
4. Building size and character is regulated to spatially define streets and squares.
5. Squares and parks are distributed and designed as specialized places for social activity and recreation.
6. Well-placed civic buildings act as symbols of the community identity and provide places for purposeful assembly.

These physical conventions pursue certain social objectives.

1. The compact organization reduces the requirements for infrastructure, automobile use, and pollution, and facilitates public transit.
2. The full range of housing types and workplaces helps to integrate all age groups and economic classes.
3. The provision of comfortable public places allows residents to come to know each other and watch over their collective security.
4. The provision of most of the necessities of daily life within walking distance allows the elderly and the young to gain independence of movement.
5. Suitable civic buildings are intended to encourage democratic initiatives and the balanced evolution of society.

ADITIONAL NEIGHBORHOOD DEVELOPEMENT ORDINANCE — PALM BEACH COUNTY, FLORIDA

PROVISIONS

F. LAND USE	G. LAND ALLOCATION	H. LOTS AND BUILDINGS	I. STREETS AND ALLEYS	J. PARKING
1. General Land Use: a. Land within a TND shall be available for uses as provided below - except those defined in the Palm Beach County Code as Prohibited Uses. b. The entire land area of a TND shall be divided into a Neighborhood Proper and Edge Areas.	**1. General Land Allocation:** a. Similar land use categories shall generally enfront across streets, dissimilar categories may abut at rear Lot lines. b. Corner Lots which enfront on Streets of dissimilar Use catagories shall be designated the category with the greater intensity of use, in descending order : HDR, LDR, Workshop.	**1. General Lots & Buildings:** a. All Lots shall share a Frontage Line with a Street or Square. b. All buildings, except Outbuildings, shall have their main entrance opening to a Street or Square . c. Stoops, open colonnades and open porches may encroach into the front setbacks. d. Building walls placed less than 5 feet from a side Lot line shall remain windowless. e. Attics and Raised Basements shall not count against the Story height limitations.	**1. General Streets & Alleys:** a. Streets shall provide access to all Tracts and Lots. b. 95% of all streets shall terminate at other streets within the TND. c. There shall generally be a continuous network of Alleys to the rear of the Lots in the TND. d. The average perimeter of all Blocks within the TND shall not exceed 1300 ft. No Block face shall have a length greater than 300 ft. (without an Alley providing through access). e. Streetlamps shall be installed on both sides of streets at no more than 100 ft. intervals - measured diagonally across the street, or parallel to the street, whichever is the greater.	**1. General Parking:** a. On-Street parking directly enfronting a Lot shall count toward fulfilling the parking requirement. b. The Master Developer may reduce the required number of parking spaces by demonstrating the possibility of Shared Parking. c. Parking Lots shall generally be located at the rear or at the side of Buildings and shall be screened from the sidewalk by Streetwalls. Shade Trees shall be installed within 4 ft. of the Frontage Line at Parking Lots at an average of 12 ft. intervals. d. Parking Lots and parking garages shall not abut Street intersections or Civic Use Lots, be adjacent to Squares or Parks, or occupy Lots which terminate a Street Vista. e. Adjacent parking Lots shall have vehicular connections, internally.
2. Public Land Use: a. Land designated for Public Use shall be Tracts containing Parks, Squares, Edge Areas, Streets and Alleys all held in common by the Property Owner's Association. b. Civic Uses may be placed within Tracts designated for Public Use. c. Large scale recreational uses such as golf courses and multiple game fields shall be located only outside the Neighborhood Proper and within the Edge Area.	**2. Public Land Allocation:** a. A minimum of five percent (5%) of the gross area of the Neighborhood or five (5) acres (whichever is greater) shall be permanently allocated to Public Use Tracts containing Squares or Parks. b. Each TND shall contain at least one Square, no less than one (1) acre in size. This Square shall be within 500 ft. of the geographic center of the Neighborhood. c. The remaining Public Use area shall be divided and distributed such that no portion of the Neighborhood is further than 500 ft. from a Park or Square. d. Squares, Parks and waterfronts if existing or provided shall have at least fifty percent (50%) of their perimeter abutting Street ROWs.	**2. Public Lots & Buildings:** a. Balconies and colonnades shall be permitted to encroach up to 4 ft. into a Public Use Tract. Such encroachments shall be protected by easements.	**2. Public Streets & Alleys:** a. Streets enfronting Public Use tracts such as Squares may deviate from the standards of the adjacent Lot types, provided the difference is intended to enhance the Public Use.	**2. Public Parking:** a. The Developer shall demonstrate the provision of adequate parking for Public Use tracts containing Squares and Parks. Shared Parking shall be encouraged for Public Uses. b. Parking Lots on Public Use tracts, shall be graded, Traditionaled and landscaped, but may be left unpaved.
3. Civic Land Use: a. Land designated for Civic Use shall be in Tracts or Lots generally containing community buildings including Meeting Halls, libraries, post offices, schools, child care centers, clubhouses, religious buildings, recreational facilities, museums, cultural societies, visual and performance arts buildings, municipal buildings and others by Special Exception. b. The ongoing construction of community buildings on Civic Lots shall be supported by a permanent assessment dedicated to that purpose and administered by the Property Owners' Association.	**3. Civic Land Allocation:** a. A minimum of two percent (2%) of the gross area of the Neighborhood shall be designated for Civic Use Lots. b. Civic Lots shall be within or adjacent to a Square or Park tract or on a Lot terminating a Street Vista. c. The Master Developer shall covenant to construct a Meeting Hall on a Civic Lot, on or adjacent to a Square, upon the sale of seventy-five percent (75%) of the Lots, for each Neighborhood of the TND. d. There shall be a Civic Lot of suitable size designated for child-care use for every 200 units planned for a Neighborhood. The Property Owner's Association shall be responsible for the organization, funding and construction of an appropriate Building on this site as the need arises.	**3. Civic Lots & Buildings:** a. Buildings located on Civic Use Lots shall be subject to no height or setback limitations.	**3. Civic Streets & Alleys:** a. Streets enfronting Civic Use Lots may deviate from the standards of the adjacent Lot types, provided the difference is intended to enhance the Civic Use.	**3. Civic Parking:** a. The Developer shall demonstrate the provision of adequate parking for the various types of Civic Buildings. Shared Parking shall be encouraged for Civic Uses. b. Parking Lots for Civic Buildings used principally on holidays must be graded, Traditionaled and planted, but may be left unpaved (i.e. religious Buildings). c. No less than 75% of the off-Street parking places for Civic Buildings shall be to the rear of the Building. Access may be through the Frontage.
4. Commercial Land Use: a. Land designated for Commercial Use shall be in Lots generally containing buildings primarily for business uses including retail, restaurant club, Corporate Office, medical, entertainment, Lodging, Artisanal, Residential and other uses by Special Exception. b. At least twenty five percent (25%) of the Net Commercial Building area shall be designated for Residential Use.	**4. Commercial Land Allocation:** a. A minimum of two percent (2%) and a maximum of thirty percent (30%) of the gross area of the Neighborhood shall be designated for Commercial Uses. b. Shopfront Use Lots shall have a maximum Frontage Line of 50 ft. c. A maximum of 5 Shopfront Lots may be consolidated for the purpose of constructing a single Building. d. Setbacks on consolidated Shopfront Lots shall apply as in a single Lot.	**4. Commercial Lots & Buildings:** a. Buildings on Commercial Use Lots shall have the Facade built within 5 ft. of the Frontage Line along at least 70% of their length. b. The unbuilt portion of the Frontage Line shall have a Streetwall built within 5 ft. of it.. c. Buildings on Commercial Use Lots shall have no setback from at least one side Lot line. d. Building Cover shall not exceed more than 70% of the Lot area. e. Buildings shall not exceed 4 Stories in height and be no less than two Stories in height. When fronting a Square, Buildings shall be no less than 3 Stories in height.	**4. Commercial Streets & Alleys:** a. Commercial Use Lots shall enfront on Streets with a maximum ROW of 70 ft, consisting of at least; two 12 ft travel lanes, 8 ft. parallel parking on both sides, and sidewalks 12 ft. wide. The Curb Radius shall not exceed 15 ft. b. Commercial Use Lots shall have their rear Lot lines coinciding with an Alley tract 24 ft. wide containing a vehicular pavement width of at least 8 ft. c. Where permitted, Commercial Use Lots may enfront on Through Streets.	**4. Commercial Parking:** a. There shall be one parking space per 300 sq. ft. of Building for restaurant, office, entertainment and Artisanal uses, one per room of lodging and one per two bedrooms of residential use. b. No less than 75 % of the parking places shall be to the rear of the Building. Access may be through the Frontage.
5. High Density Residential Land Use: a. Land designated for HDR Use shall be in Lots generally containing buildings for residential and limited business uses including townhouse, Apartment, Coffee House, Limited Office, Limited Lodging, Artisanal and other uses by Special Exception. b. One hundred percent (100%) of the Net Building area above the ground floor shall be designated for residential use. c. An Outbuilding is permitted on each Lot.	**5. High Density Residential Land Allocation:** a. A minimum of fifteen percent (15%) and a maximum of thirty percent (30%) of the gross area of the Neighborhood shall be designated for HDR Uses. b. HDR Use Lots shall have a maximum Frontage Line of 50 ft. c. A maximum of 12 HDR Lots may be consolidated for the purpose of constructing a single Building containing Apartments equal in number to the Lots consolidated. e. Setbacks on consolidated HDR Lots shall apply as in a single Lot.	**5. High Density Residential Lots & Buildings:** a. Buildings on HDR Use Lots shall be setback either 5ft or 15 ft. from the Frontage Line. Buildings at Street intersections shall be setback 5 ft. from both Frontage Lines. b. Buildings shall have no required setbacks from the side Lot lines. c. Building Cover shall not exceed more than 70% of the Lot area. d. Buildings shall not exceed 3 Stories in height. e. Buildings shall have a Streetedge built along the unbuilt portion of the Frontage Line.	**5. High Density Residential Streets & Alleys:** a. HDR Use Lots shall enfront on Streets with a maximum ROW of 50 ft, consisting of at least; two 10 ft. travel lanes, 7 ft parallel parking on both sides, and sidewalks 6 ft. wide. The Curb Radius shall not exceed 15 ft. b. Street Trees shall be installed on both sides of HDR Streets at no more than 75 ft. intervals - measured diagonally across, or parallel to, the Street - whichever is greater. c. HDR Lots shall have their rear Lot lines coinciding with an Alley 24 ft. wide containing a vehicular pavement width of at least 8 ft.	**5. High Density Residential Parking:** a. There shall be one parking place per 300 sq. ft. of commercial, one per room of lodging and one per two bedrooms of residential use. b. All off-Street parking places shall be to the rear of the Building. Access shall be through an Alley only.
6. Low Density Residential Land Use: a. Land designated for LDR Use shall be in Lots generally containing buildings for residential and uses including single family houses, artist studios, guest cottages, Home Office, Limited Lodging and others by Special Exception. b. One hundred percent (100%) of the Building area above the ground floor shall be designated for residential use. c. An Outbuilding is permitted on each Lot.	**6. Low Density Residential Land Allocation:** a. A maximum of forty percent (40%) of the gross area of the Neighborhood shall be designated for LDR Use. b. LDR Use Lot shall have a maximum Frontage Line of 75 ft. c. A maximum of two LDR Lots may be consolidated for the purpose of constructing a single Building. d. Setbacks on consolidated LDR Lots shall apply as in a single Lot.	**6. Low Density Residential Lots & Buildings:** a. Buildings on LDR Lots shall be setback between 0 and 25 ft. from the Frontage Line. b. Buildings shall be setback from the side Lot lines equivalent (in total) to no less than 20% of the width of the Lot. The entire setback may be allocated to one side. c. Buildings shall be setback no less than 30 ft. from the rear Lot line except for outbuildings. d. Building Cover shall not exceed more than 70% of the Lot area. e. Buildings on shall not exceed 2 Stories in height. f. Buildings shall have a Streetedge along the unbuilt portion of the Frontage Line.	**6. Low Density Residential Streets & Alleys:** a. LDR Use Lots shall enfront on Streets with a maximum ROW of 50 ft, consisting of at least; two 8 ft. travel lanes, and sidewalk 4 ft. wide. The Curb Radius shall not exceed 25 ft.. b. Shade Trees shall be installed on both sides of the Street at no more than 150 ft. intervals - measured diagonally across the Street, or parallel to the Street, whichever is the greater. c. LDR Use Lots may have their rear Lot lines coinciding with an Alley tract 24 ft. wide.	**6. Low Density Residential Parking:** a. There shall be one parking place per 300 sq. ft. of office, one per room of lodging and one per two bedrooms of residential use. b. All off-Street parking places shall be to the side or the rear of the Building. Where access is through the Frontage, garages or carports shall be located a minimum of 20 feet behind the Facade.
7. Workshop Land Use: a. Land designated for Workshop Use shall be in lots generally containing Buildings for Corporate Office, Light Industry, Artisanal, Warehousing,Automotive, and others by Special Exception.	**7. Workshop Land Allocation :** a. A minimum of two percent (2%) and a maximum of thirty percent (30%) of the gross area of the Neighborhood shall be designated for Workshop Uses. b. Workshop Use Lots shall have a maximum Frontage Line of 100 ft. c. A maximum of two Workshop Use Lots may be consolidated for the purpose of constructing a single Building. d. Workshop Use Lots shall not be closer to the geographic center of the Neighborhood or the mandatory Square than 300 ft. - or one- third the depth of the Neighborhood. e. Workshop Use Lots shall generally be grouped together.	**7. Workshop Lots & Buildings:** a. Buildings on Workshop Use Lots shall not require setbacks from front or side Lot lines. b. Buildings Cover shall not exceed more than 70% of the Lot area. c. Buildings shall not exceed 2 Stories in height. d. Workshop Use Lots shall be separated from other use types at the side and rear Lot lines (excepting an entry on the Alley) by a continuous masonry wall no less than 10 ft. in height.	**7. Workshop Streets & Alleys:** a. Workshop Use Lots shall enfront on Streets with a maximum ROW of 65 ft, consisting of at least; two 11 ft. travel lanes, one 10 ft. central turning lane, parallel parking on both sides and sidewalks 6 ft. wide. The Curb Radius shall not exceed 25 ft . b. Where permitted, Lots may also enfront Through Streets. c. Lots shall have their rear Lot lines coinciding with an Alley tract 24 ft. wide containing a vehicular pavement width of at least 8 ft.	**7. Workshop Parking:** a. There shall be one parking place per 500 sq. ft. of Building, except Corporate Office Use, which shall have one per 300 sq. ft. b. Off-Street parking places may be to one side or to the rear of the Building.

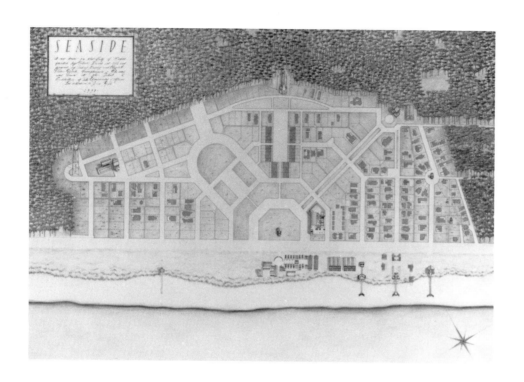

Patrick Pinnell

Organon

Seaside has many fences but no Fence. It is a little community whose chief planner was not Robert Davis or Andres Duany or Elizabeth Plater-Zyberk but, secretly, Aristotle. One can imagine Aristotle strolling through Seaside in the raking light of cocktail hour, chatting across fences with people on porches. They would admire his *chiton* and tan; he their easy civility.

This is to say that there is not only a theory of urbanism at work at Seaside and the places seen here, but a way of thinking about the world—an Aristotelian preference for providing models rather than Platonic, absolute types. Seaside's fences may be the best emblem of this thinking. For Aristotle, types existed only as they materialized in individual instances, and every new instance subtly shifted the centerline of the type.

For the long run this will be the significance of Duany and Plater-Zyberk's towns, more than the aspects more often under discussion: the doubts raised about just how benign their for-profit developers can become; the questions voiced concerning just how authentic, as "art" and as places to live, these things are; and especially the distaste expressed by with-it designers and students (more than by real people) for the styles of individual buildings and the perceived restrictions on creativity imposed by the codes.

It is useful to situate the work of Andres Duany and Elizabeth Plater-Zyberk by thinking about their thinking, not so much to evaluate the criticism which it seems to draw from otherwise mutually antagonistic quarters, but more as a tactic for understanding, by comparisons, the means and forms they use and the social and political critique they make. For, despite the "Neotraditionalist" label which often stamps their work, and regardless of the long looks it takes at past styles and building types, old suburbs, and older towns, the work is a truly odd amalgam of nostalgia and uncenteredness. In fact it ought to discomfort not only Modernists and Post-Structuralists but party-line Classicists too, if they would only get beyond the warm fuzzies brought on by the perspective drawings and into the urbanism delineated and the politics implied.

One demonstration of a characteristic Duany and Plater-Zyberk tactic will show why. Their public presentations inevitably carry a segment on the visual, practical, and social evils of cul-de-sac "pod" developments, proposing instead the virtues of the old-fashioned, continuous rectilinear grid. It is interesting then to look at any one of the thirty-something town plans they've produced and find that—while one is nicely guided at the ground level between one place and another—the whole is like no grid ever sponsored by Thomas Jefferson. Instead we find ourselves looking at something more like Piranesi's imaginary Campus Martius, or what's left, after the last breakfast bowlful, at the bottom of a Rice Chex box.

Such frayed patchwork grids reveal that in Duany and Plater-Zyberk's planning, order means local order, usually very local indeed. This is equally true of the smaller plans and the bigger ones. Deerfield, at 40 acres, has three discernible centers. Mashpee Commons, at 450 acres, has five or six. Over its 1600 acres, Wellington has seven or eight strong little formal force fields dispersed. Even there though, the local orders are not of ideal geometries, in contrast, say, to Griffin and Mahoney's Canberra plan, where each of the several centers is a spider throwing out an octagonal web of streets. Mashpee's circles receive due radial respect from the larger roads leading into them but are barely recognized by their neighboring residential streets and squares. This makes for places that are easily legible and navigable on the ground, but very hard to hold as *overall* patterns in the memory.

Related to this are the ways that the blocks marked out by streets are handled, and the ways that civic buildings and structures of collective significance are located and used. Formalizing earlier tendencies, the later project presentations have begun to feature a sheet showing a "standard block," with individual property lines and alleys laid down. But go to the overall plan and almost never is such a block actually present, much less serially repeated Manhattan-style. Though still recognizable, the blocks are bent, squeezed, stretched, chopped, or inflected expediently to suit terrain, orientation, or what have you in the way of local circumstance. This is done so consistently that it must be regarded as evidence of more than a desire to simulate the grown-up-over-time patterns of smaller, pre-Western Reserve Act American towns. Duany and Plater-Zyberk seem to avoid absolute didactic insistence on the presence of any pure thing or form. Again, Aristotle prevails.

Pronounced localism further reveals their underlying social and political attitudes in the case of collective-use structures. All of Duany and Plater-Zyberk's master plans, new towns, redevelopments, and restorations contain, and specifically locate, churches, little as-yet-undedicated monuments, post offices, high schools, and the like—all of them structures which suggest affiliation with causes or institutions larger than the community being designed. On inspection, the placement of these usually does not suggest the same degree of logic demonstrated in the placement of a different sort of communal structure, such as day care centers or grade schools, which serve specific local needs.

The civic spaces with which the civic structures consort are usually designed in great detail, in current projects down to the species and intervals of trees. The varieties of housing, too, are identified and considerably worked on as to specific logical reciprocities between urban situation and internal planning. The generic quality of the monuments is in such contrast to the specificity of proposals for public spaces and the private realm that one must suspect a cause more significant than the attentiveness induced by the developer's making his or her money mostly from the houses, and more theory-connected than is suggested by the standard Duany and Plater-Zyberk practice of usually arranging to have these buildings designed in detail later, by other architects, long after the manic charrettes which produce the town plan and its initial illustrations.

One possible explanation is that these monumental structures really no longer house institutions which are regarded in the traditional ways. The church at Deerfield might behave in an urban way very much like Latrobe's Monumental Church in Charleston, but there is still somehow a sense of difference. These porticoes and steeples, obelisks and tempiettos wig-wag motorists around quite well and will make for great postcard views, but the aura of their representing dominative things in the life of the community is absent. The mindset of the traditional American town when it was founded was more often that the houses were built to support the church than that the church was built to be a convenience for the houses. Monumental buildings were literally moral admonitions, as the etymology reveals: *ad monere*—towards memory—specifically memory of those beliefs, values, and forms of behavior which were demanded by institutions of those within their fields of power. In the Duany and Plater-Zyberk plans it is very hard to discern a hierarchy of monuments, the sorting out of degrees of power to be expected when institutions still exert, and compete for, control—a hierarchy often quite legible in historic town plans. This is not to say that the institutions housed in such structures will not be important to the lives of those living in Duany and Plater-Zyberk settlements. Rather, they will be used as, and the planners have treated them as, nothing either less or more than another variety of local community facility.

To point this out is not to suggest that the planners are unauthentic; if anything, just the opposite is intended. Disempowerment of the monuments can be looked at mistakenly as simply giving in, as ratification of the busy, unprincipled, consumerist reality of contemporary American culture. Though generic in a way that, once understood, is logically appropriate to how it is likely to function, the Duany and Plater-Zyberk monument, like that typical Duany and Plater-Zyberk block, is realized only in inflected form, in a different but consistent tactic to make over any extracommunal idea into a strictly local order. This would seem to make the work susceptible instead, ironically, to the critique which says that now there are still institutions in control, and that just because they are different, invisible, nonparticipatory, and elsewhere, does not make them any less powerful.

Now things get really interesting. For, both in what they say directly and even more by what they leave as an implication, Duany and Plater-Zyberk are concerned with wresting back a degree of local order on this front too. By deemphasizing the use of the automobile, they reduce the control of those outside interests which corrode autonomy and induce economic dependence; not only the automobile industry, but the oil and gas consortia; the highway lobby; the banks, which gladly lend money for an expense likely to be repeated every five years. It is not a matter of completely declaring, or wanting, independence, but of reasserting balance. By demanding, and often receiving, control of the codes for the areas they're working on, Duany and Plater-Zyberk can bring about a certain local emancipation. It is not a long conceptual leap to other steps, such as stipulations that savings and loan institutions place local savings in local investments rather than being allowed to ship money out to "opportunities" halfway across the country or the world.

The work here shown, in short, attempts to discover a classic urbanism which yet does not pretend to represent perfection or universality of formal and social order and which seeks to displace institutions, at least partially, from their monopolistic control over the possibility of difference, over the relationship between individual lives and the world. In *Ethics*, Aristotle judged that no single political state should exceed a certain size; by extension consistent with his thinking, none should become either too powerful or too abstractly ordered. Eventually successful or eventually failing, Duany and Plater-Zyberk's towns are in that tradition of thinking. Theirs is work with a high degree of consistency in its technical means, in its chosen and invented forms, and in its consciously intended ends.

Patrick Pinnell is an architect and Associate Professor of Architecture at Yale University.

APPENDICES

Andres Duany and Elizabeth Plater-Zyberk

Andres Duany and Elizabeth Plater-Zyberk completed undergraduate studies in architecture at Princeton and both went on to receive the master's degree in architecture from Yale in 1974. They have lived in Miami since 1975 where they teach in the University of Miami Master of Architecture Program in Suburb and Town Design.

Mr. Duany and Ms. Plater-Zyberk maintain an architectural practice in Miami which continues an exploration of Caribbean architecture; they have completed over 20 buildings in the last ten years. Their town planning practice, pursued in Miami as well as in outpost offices in Boston and near Washington, D.C., has produced over 30 new town and urban revitalization plans, six of which are under construction, and one of which is largely built. Their practice includes writing codes for the new towns and for existing municipalities.

VILLAGES

A Village Near Annapolis

Bill Lennertz
Charles Barrett
Frank Martinez

A Settlement at Sandy Spring

Bill Lennertz
Charles Barrett
Warren Byrd
Juan Caruncho
Chester Chellman
Manuel Fernandez-Noval
Geoff Ferrell
Michael Franck
Elizabeth Guyton
Neal Payton
Mike Watkins
Kamal Zaharin

Windsor

Geoff Ferrell
Hector Valverde
Charles Barrett
Juan Caruncho
Peter Jefferson
Robert Trent Jones, Jr.
Dony Marin
Scott Merrill
Desmond Muirhead
Tarik El Naggar
Felix Pereira
Craig Roberts
Estela Valle
Kamal Zaharin

Tannin

Frank Martinez
Charles Barrett
Jay Cameron
Juan Caruncho
Keller Easterling
Manuel Fernandez-Noval
Randall Maingot
Erick Valle
Estela Valle
Meor Zulaidin

TOWNS AND CITIES

Belmont

Bill Lennertz
Elizabeth Guyton
Steven Van Gorp
Charles Barrett
Chester Chellman
William Dennis
Tarik El Naggar
Manuel Fernandez-Noval
Scott Fritz
Jay Gordon
Jay Graham
Paul Hurney
Klaus Ising
Sarah Ivetich
Don Johnson
Rich McLaughlin
Scott Merrill
Patrick Pinnell
Max Underwood
Hector Valverde
Mike Watkins
David Wolfe

Haymount

Mike Watkins
Andres Batista
Matt Bell
Warren Byrd
Chester Chellman
Manuel Fernandez-Noval
Geoff Ferrell
Michael Franck
Elizabeth Guyton
Chip Kaufman
Brian Kelley
Bill Lennertz
Neil Payton
Tom Spain
Kamal Zaharin

Capital City Renaissance

Ted Liebman
Alan Melting
Frank Martinez
Steven Van Gorp
Charles Barrett
Bill Lennertz
Alick McLean
Kevin Smith
Estela Valle

Kentlands

Bill Lennertz
Mike Watkins
Charles Barrett
Keith Bowers
Chester Chellman
Raymond Chu
William Dennis
Douglas Duany
Tarik El Naggar
Manuel Fernandez-Noval
Jay Graham
Alex Krieger
Doug La Rosa
Mark Lucy
Leon Nitzin
Patrick Pinnell
Kathy Poole
Dhiru Thadani
Estela Valle
David Wolfe

Wellington

Scott Hedge
Charles Barrett
Chester Chellman
Manuel Fernandez-Noval
Geoff Ferrell
Jorge Hernandez
Chip Kaufman
Jean-Francois LeJeune
Ralph Portuondo
Jorge Trelles
Luis Trelles
Kristin Triff
Kamal Zaharin

Mashpee Commons

Bill Lennertz
Charles Barrett
Stephane Bothwell
Chester Chellman
William Dennis
Douglas Duany
Tarik El Naggar
Manuel Fernandez-Noval
Scott Hedge
Alex Krieger
John Montague Massengale
Alick McLean
Douglas Storrs
Ann Tate

TERRITORIES

Blount Springs

Frank Martinez
Juan Caruncho
Charles Barrett
Ernesto Buch
Edah Grover
John Harrison
Bill Lennertz
Suzanne Singleton
Estela Valle

Nance Canyon

Chip Kaufman
Scott Hedge
Charles Barrett
Andres Batista
Edward Blakeley
Steward Brand
Victoria Casasco
Walter Chatham
Chester Chellman
Gary Coates
Ronald Crites
Kerry Dawson
Elizabeth Deakin
William Dennis
Stephen Finn
Manuel Fernandez-Noval
Geoff Ferrell
James Jokertz
Bill Lennertz
Cecelia Kapitan
Pam Kinzie
Jay Oschrin
David Prasitka
Ellis Rolls
William Shireman
Barbara Stauffacher-Solomon
Tom Spain
Robert Thayer
Kamal Zaharin
James Zanetto
Len Zegarski

Avalon Park

Hector Valverde
Carlos Aparicio
Charles Barrett
Andres Batista
Chester Chellman
Manuel Fernandez-Noval
Geoff Ferrell
Scott Hedge
Chip Kaufman
Jean-Francois LeJeune
Rodolfo Machado
Rich McLaughlin
Grace Perdomo
Iskandar Shafie
Jorge Trelles
Luis Trelles
Kamal Zaharin

CHARLESTON PLACE
Boca Raton, Florida

Joseph Homes Company
16-acre residential community
Site plan, design of five unit types,
construction documents
Designed 1980
Construction completed 1986

SEASIDE
Santa Rosa Beach, Florida

Robert Davis
80-acre new town
Site master plan, zoning code,
design regulations, supervision
Designed 1982
Under construction

TANNIN
Orange Beach, Alabama

George Gounares & Associates, Inc.
60-acre new town
Site master plan, zoning code,
design regulations, building design,
supervision
Designed 1986
Under construction

FRIDAY MOUNTAIN
Austin, Texas

Whitehawk Development Corporation
500-acre new town
Site master plan, zoning code,
design regulations
Designed 1987
Unbuilt

BEDFORD THREE CORNERS
Bedford, New Hampshire

HABS Company
120-acre residential community
Site master plan, zoning code,
design regulations
Designed 1987
Unbuilt

BOWMAN'S GREEN
Bedford, New Hampshire

HABS Company
14-acre residential neighborhood
Site master plan, zoning code,
design regulations
Designed 1987
Unbuilt

DISNEY PROTOTYPICAL TOWN
Osceola County, Florida

Disney Development Corporation
2,500-acre new town
Site master plan, zoning code,
design regulations
Designed 1988
Redesigned by others

BLOUNT SPRINGS
Blount Springs, Alabama

Blount Springs Recolonization Partners, Inc.
5,000-acre new town
Site master plan, zoning code,
design regulations
Building design, construction documents,
supervision
Designed 1988
Under construction

MUNCIE
Muncie, Indiana

City of Muncie
10-mile corridor of Route 332
Site master plan,
implementation strategies
Designed 1988
Under continuing study

A VILLAGE NEAR ANNAPOLIS
Anne Arundel County, Maryland

Owner's name withheld
174-acre residential community
Site master plan, zoning code,
design regulations
Designed 1988
Redesigned by others

STURBRIDGE
Rochester, New York

GMA Development
58-acre residential community
Site master plan, zoning code,
design regulations
Designed 1988
Unbuilt

DEERFIELD
Merrillville, Indiana

Executive Park Limited
40-acre new town
Site master plan, zoning code,
design regulations
Designed 1988
Project on hold

ST. LUCIE WEST
Port St. Lucie, Florida

Thomas White Corporation
4,500-acre new town
Site master plan, zoning code,
design regulations
Designed 1988
Redesigned by others

KENTLANDS
Gaithersburg, Maryland

Joseph Alfandre & Company, Inc.
356-acre new town
Site master plan, zoning code, design
regulations, building design, supervision
Designed 1988
Under construction

STUART
Stuart, Florida

City of Stuart
800-acre Downtown Redevelopment Plan
Site master plan, zoning code,
street standards, implementation strategies
Designed 1988
Under construction

MASHPEE COMMONS
Mashpee, Massachusetts

Fields Point Limited Partnership, owner
Arnold B. Chace, Jr., developer
278-acre new town center
Site master plan, zoning code,
design regulations, supervision
Designed 1988
Under construction

MARINELAND
Flagler County, Florida

Marineland of Florida, Inc.
140-acre new town
Site master plan, zoning code,
design regulations, environmental
impact statement
Designed 1988
Permits pending

BELMONT
Loudoun County, Virginia

Joseph Alfandre & Company, Inc.
273-acre new town
Site master plan, zoning code,
design regulations, supervision
Designed 1988
Permitted

SHORESIDE VILLAGES
Eastern Shore, Virginia

Owner's name withheld
330-acre and 420-acre residential communities
Site master plan, zoning code,
design regulations
Designed 1988
Project on hold

SANDY SPRING
Sandy Spring, Maryland

Joseph Alfandre & Company, Inc.
400-acre new town
Site master plan, zoning code,
design regulations
Designed 1988
Permits pending

CAPITAL CITY RENAISSANCE
Trenton, New Jersey

Capital City Redevelopment Corporation
640-acre urban redevelopment
Master plan, zoning code,
design regulations
Designed 1989
Under construction

SOUTH HILL
Ithaca, New York

Auble Metropolis Group
325-acre new town
Site master plan, zoning code,
design regulations
Designed 1989
Project on hold

WINDSOR
Vero Beach, Florida

Westnor Limited and
Abercrombie & Kent Int'l., Inc.
400-acre residential community
Site master plan, zoning code,
design regulations, supervision
Designed 1989
Under construction

PLAYA VISTA
Los Angeles, California

Maguire Thomas Partners
900-acre urban development
Site master plan, zoning code,
design regulations, supervision
With Moore, Ruble, Yudell; Ricardo Legorreta;
de Brettville and Polyzoides; Hanna and Olin
Designed 1989
Permits pending

RIVERLANDS
Bedford, New Hampshire

HABS Company
100-acre new town
Site master plan, zoning code,
design regulations
Designed 1989
Redesigned by others

INGRAHAM CORNER
West Rockport, Maine

Rockport TND, Inc.
100-acre new town
Site master plan, zoning code,
design regulations
Designed 1989
Permits pending

NICHOLSON QUARTER
Williamsburg, Virginia

Nicholson Quarter Company
28-acre, 125-unit affordable, mixed-income
residential community
Site master plan, zoning code,
design regulations
Designed 1989
Unbuilt

SAILBOAT BEND
Fort Lauderdale, Florida

Sailboat Bend Homeowners Association
180-acre growth plan for
existing urban community
Site master plan, zoning code,
design regulations
Designed 1989
Under construction

POUNDBURY
Dorchester, Dorset, England

Duchy of Cornwall
400-acre village designed by Leon Krier
Zoning code, design regulations
Designed 1989
Permits pending

WELLINGTON
Palm Beach County, Florida

Corepoint Corporation
1,500-acre new town
Site master plan, zoning code,
design regulations, supervision
Designed 1989
Permits pending

HAYMOUNT
Caroline County, Virginia

Haymount Limited Partnership, owner
Robertson and Clark, developers
1,582-acre new town
Site master plan, zoning code,
design regulations, supervision
Designed 1989
Permits pending

AVALON PARK
Orlando, Florida

Flag Development Company, Inc.
9,400-acre regional plan
Site master plan, zoning code,
design regulations, supervision
Designed 1989
Permits pending

RANCHO DEL SOL
Martin County, Florida

Divosta and Company
2,700-acre new town
Site master plan, design regulations
Designed 1990
Unbuilt

THE GATE DISTRICT
St. Louis, Missouri

City of St. Louis
440-acre urban neighborhood restoration
Site master plan, housing code, prototypes
Designed 1990
Permits pending

NASSAU FOREST
Fernandina Beach, Florida

Embry Burney Inc.
586-acre new town
Site master plan, design regulations
Preliminary design 1990
Project on hold

NANCE CANYON
Chico, California

Blakeley Swartz, owner
Tom DiGiovanni, developer
Steve Honeycutt, developer
3,050-acre new town
Site master plan, zoning code,
design regulations
Designed 1990
Permits pending

1980

Tigerman, Stanley. *Late Entries to the Chicago Tribune Tower Competition.* New York: Rizzoli International Publications, Inc., 1980.

1982

Plater-Zyberk, Elizabeth. "O'Connell House/Charleston Place." *Werk, Bauen + Wohnen Nr. 5,* May 1982, pp. 20–21.

1983

Gandee, Charles K. "Hibiscus House, Coconut Grove, Florida." *Architectural Record,* May 1983, pp. 102–105.

1984

Burns, Carol J. "New Work: 10 Architects." *Perspecta 21,* 1984, pp. 80–99.

Doubilet, Susan. "The Town of Seaside." *Progressive Architecture,* January 1984, pp. 138–139.

Sachner, Paul M. "Punta Alegre, Key Biscayne, Florida." *Architectural Record,* April 1984, pp. 70–73.

Gualteri, Franca Santi. "In Florida: A House With a Loggia." *Abitare,* April 1984, pp. 12–17.

Porphyrios, Demetri, ed. "Galen Medical Building." *Architectural Design Profile 53,* May/June 1984, pp. 56–57.

Porphyrios, Demetri, ed. "Vilanova House, Florida." *Architectural Design Profile 53,* May/June 1984, pp 66–67.

Porphyrios, Demetri, ed. "De la Cruz House." *Architectural Design Profile 53,* May/June 1984, pp. 72–73.

Doubilet, Susan. "A Venerable Town Pattern Reemerges." *Progressive Architecture,* August 1984, pp. 74–80.

Krier, Leon. "The Reconstruction of Vernacular Buildings and Classical Architecture." *The Architects' Journal,* September 12, 1984, pp. 55–84.

Greer, Diane D. "1984 FA/AIA Awards For Excellence In Architecture." *Florida Architect.* November/December 1984, pp. 13–37.

1985

Duany, Andres and Plater-Zyberk, Elizabeth. "The Town of Seaside." *The Princeton Journal: Thematic Studies in Architecture, Volume Two,* 1985, pp. 44–50.

Peters, Paulhans. "Stadhauser in Boca Raton, Florida." *e + p Wohnen,* 1985, pp.49–51.

Speck, Lawrence W. "Single Family Housing." *Center Volume 1,* 1985, pp. 102–117.

Doubilet, Susan. "32nd Annual P/A Awards." *Progressive Architecture,* January 1985, pp. 83–130.

Russell, Frank, ed. "Seaside/Hibiscus House, Florida." *Architectural Design,* January/February 1985, pp. 70–77.

Greer, Nora Richter. "Some Recent Works of Minority Architects." *Architecture,* April 1985, pp. 62–71.

Ivy, Robert A., Jr. "Building by the Sea: The Southeast." *Architecture,* June 1985, pp. 70–75.

Boles, Daralice D. "Robert Davis: Small Town Entrepreneur." *Progressive Architecture,* July 1985, pp. 111–118.

Greer, Diane. "1985 FA/AIA Awards For Excellence In Architecture." *Florida Architect,* September/October 1985, pp. 23–37.

1986

Duany, Andres. "De la Cruz House." *Cuban Architects,* 1985/1986, pp. 29–31.

Duany, Andres. "Principles in the Architecture of Alvar Aalto." *Harvard Architecture Review 5,* 1986, pp. 104–119.

Allen, Gerald. *Emerging Voices.* Princeton, NJ: Princeton University Press, 1986.

Abrams, Janet. "The Form of the (American) City." *Lotus International 50,* 1986, pp. 7–29.

Doubilet, Susan. "Classical Abstractions." *Progressive Architecture,* April 1986, pp. 101–103.

Sachner, Paul M. "Temperate Zone: Vilanova House, Key Biscayne, Florida." *Architectural Record,* April 1986, pp. 134–139.

Nesmith, Lynn. "AIA Component Awards." *Architecture,* May 1986, pp. 66–259.

Anton, Frank. "Builder's Best: The New Town, The Old Ways." *Builder,* July 1986, pp. 60–65.

Ochsner, Jeffrey Karl. "The Past In Our Future." *Texas Architect,* July/August 1986, pp. 38–47.

Peters, Paulhans. "Die Ferienstadt Seaside in Florida, USA." *Baumeister 9,* September 1986, pp. 60–67.

Stern, Robert, A.M. *Pride of Place: Building the American Dream.* Boston: Houghton Mifflin Company, 1986.

Stockman, Leslie Ensor. "1986 Builder's Choice Design Awards." *Builder,* October 1986, pp. 130–188.

Sachner, Paul M. "Punta Alegre/Vilanova House, Key Biscayne, Florida." *Architectural Record: The Record Houses Collection, 1984/1985/1986,* pp. 70–73 and 134–139.

1987

Duany, Andres. "Teaching Design En Loge." *Zero Hour,* 1987.

Greer, Nora Richter. "Desperate Efforts To Shape Florida's Runaway Growth." *Architecture,* April 1987, pp. 56–63.

Langdon, Philip. *American Houses.* New York: Stewart, Tabori & Chang, Inc., 1987.

Barnett, Jonathan. "In The Public Interest: Design Guidelines." *Architectural Record*, July 1987, pp. 114–125.

Sachner, Paul M. "Villa By The Bay." *Architectural Record*, sup. July 1987, pp. 80–83.

Schumacher, Thomas. "Regional Intentions and Contemporary Architecture: A Critique." *Center Volume 3*, 1987, pp. 52–59.

"Critical Speculation: Seminar IV." *Harvard Architecture Review 6*, 1987, pp. 132–135.

Harwell, Maurice. *Retrospecta 1986–1987*. Hamden, Connecticut: E.H. Roberts Printers, 1987.

Hatton, Hap. *Tropical Splendor: An Architectural History of Florida*. New York: Alfred A. Knopf, 1987.

Fuller, Larry Paul. "A New Town for Friday Mountain." *Progressive Architecture*, October 1987, pp. 33–34.

1988

American Academy in Rome: Annual Exhibition. Rome: Arti Grafiche Jasillo, 1988.

Duany, Andres and Plater-Zyberk, Elizabeth. "Andres Duany, Elizabeth Plater-Zyberk." *Metamorfosi 6–7*, September 1988, pp. 70–75.

Stern, Robert A.M. *Modern Classicism*. New York: Rizzoli, 1988.

Jencks, Charles. *Post-Modernism*. New York: Rizzoli, 1988.

Hamblen, Matt. "The Kentlands Charrette." *Urban Land*, September 1988, pp. 10–15.

Russell, James S. "Back To Neighborhood Basics." *Architectural Record*, November 1988, p. 53.

Scully, Vincent. *American Architecture and Urbanism*. New York: Henry Holt and Company, 1988.

Steil, Lucien. *Architectural Design Profile 75: Imitation & Innovation*. New York: St. Martin's Press. 1988.

1989

Pirson, Roselyn. "Le Prince et les Architectes." *La Cite*, February 16, 1989, pp. XVII–XVIII.

Pinnell, Patrick L. "The Kentlands Experiment." *Museum & Arts Washington*, March/April 1989, pp. 81–84.

Oppenheimer, Todd. "Dinosaurs Haunt Our Landscape." *Utne Reader*, March/April 1989, pp. 96–97.

Sachner, Paul M. "Common Sense." *Architectural Record*, March 1989, pp. 84–89.

Feireiss, Kristin. *14 X Amerika-Gedenkbibliothek*. Berlin: Ernst & Sohn, 1989.

Boles, Daralice D. "Reordering The Suburbs." *Progressive Architecture*, May 1989, pp. 78–91.

Melvin, Jeremy. "Creative Coding." *RIBA Journal: Building Design*, June 2, 1989.

Dunlop, Beth. "Coming of Age." *Architectural Record*, July 1989, pp. 96–101.

Santi, Carlo. "Seaside: The Small City." *Abitare*, July/August 1989, pp. 174–183.

Knack, Ruth. "Repent, Ye Sinners, Repent." *Planning*, August 1989, pp. 4–13.

Langdon, Philip. "Beyond the Cul-de-Sac." *Landscape Architecture*, October 1989, pp. 72–73.

Davis, Robert S. "Special Feature: Seaside." *Global Architecture 27*, November 1989, pp. 90–97.

Shoshkes, Ellen. *The Design Process*. New York: Watson-Guptill Publications, 1989.

Torre, L. Azeo. *Waterfront Development*. New York: Van Nostrand Reinhold, 1989.

Listokin, David. *The Subdivision and Site Plan Handbook*. New Jersey: Center For Urban Research, 1989.

Sudjic, Deyan. *From Matt Black to Memphis and Back Again*. London: Architecture Design and Technology Press, 1989.

Architectural Design Profile 81: Reconstruction Deconstruction. New York: St. Martin's Press, 1989.

1990

Pearson, Clifford A. "Conference Updates: The Call of Nature." *Architectural Record*, January 1990, pp. 25–27.

Leccese, Michael. "Next Stop: Transit-Friendly Towns." *Landscape Architecture*, July 1990, pp. 47–53.

Guroff, Margaret. "Neotraditionalism," *Home Design*, Fall 1990, pp. 36–43.

Anderson, Kurt and Jencks, Charles. "Architectural Dialogue: Charles Jencks and Kurt Anderson on the Postmodern Legacy." *Architectural Digest*, December 1990, pp. 31–40.

Lorenz, Clare. *"Women in Architecture."* London: Trefoil Publications, Ltd., 1990.

Broadbent, Geoffrey. *Emerging Concepts in Urban Space Design*. London: Van Nostrand Reinhold International, 1990.

1991

Patton, Phil. "In Seaside, Florida, The Forward Thing Is To Look Backward." *Smithsonian*, January 1991, pp. 82–93.

Scully, Vincent. "Back to the Future, With a Detour Through Miami." *The New York Times*, January 27, 1991, p. H-32.

Flanagan, Barbara. "A Massachusetts Mall is Just Disappeared." *The New York Times*, March 14, 1991, p. B-5.

If the people seem to have but little faith it is because they have been tricked so long; they are weary of dishonesty; more weary than they know; much more weary than you know. The American people are now in a stupor; be on hand at the awakening.

Louis Sullivan, 1906

Leon Krier

Afterword

Earthworks for roads, railway tracks, and airstrips may be the only twentieth-century structures to survive into future centuries. Our era will then be remembered merely as the age of mass movement: travel, circulation, transport, migration, commuting. Our own understanding of the good life and freedom is now inextricably linked to artificial means of transport and communication. As a result, few people are free to be without such means should they want to work, to educate themselves, to holiday, to retire, or simply to live.

The time, space, and energy invested in building and updating circulation infrastructures leave very little to invest in the places we actually travel to and from. For several decades now, movement has taken precedence over place.

Duany and Plater-Zyberk's work has above all to do with the creation of an American public realm, the building of places—and it is not by chance that in their continent-wide crusade they are facing square on the institutions and sacred cows of transport and circulation.

Aesthetic, ecological, communal, and civic interests as formulated in the Traditional Neighborhood Development (TND) codes are the cornerstone of true urban communities. Hierarchically they are superior to the concerns of the departments of transportation. Yet the form and content of urban development is now shaped largely by transportation policies. These policies can, in my opinion, regain proper civic purpose and meaning only when they are subordinated to a larger ecological and communal project such as the TND.

The Public Realm and the Nature of Place
Movement is an essential expression of life. In fact, before mechanization takes command, human beings move around more by their own bodily means, not less, the fundamental difference being that they move within a continuum of natural and man-made places.

Enclosed mechanical means of transport instead move us from place to place, with the area between perceived as transit limbo. That is why from early on buildings turned their backs on rail tracks, motorways, and airfields, as if they were "nonplaces." The functional zoning of cities which is made possible by artificial means of transport and communication fragments towns and landscapes into zones not only of single use but, more perniciously, of single meaning, separated by vast zones of "in-between" or "nowhere."

Instead of merely speeding up movement between places and thus extending our perception of the public realm, the mechanization of transport has so far led to the fragmentation of the very idea of place as public realm.

A true place is by nature complex, hierarchical, polyfunctional, individual, and multiform. A functional zone instead is by nature simplex, nonhierarchical, and uniform, without true identity and individuality. A true nonplace is not more than the sum of its parts.

In totalitarian regimes this crude system creates a nakedly brutal environment. In democratic systems, nonplaces are often spontaneously given an ersatz identity, resulting in kitsch-reality, clipped of meaning; they are travesties of places, skin-deep architecture, lived in by phony communities.

An L.A. student succinctly described this phenomenon: "Americans are not really at home in any place; neither at home, nor at work, nor at the club or the shopping mall. They are truly at home only when moving from one place to another."

Paradoxically, the United States is a vast country with very few true places. Zoning and the exponential explosion of populations and towns has not only resulted in countless new nonplaces and in-betweens; they have profoundly eroded existing places, which have almost without exception been transformed into heritage consumer items; state sets to be looked at, at best to be lived in on weekends.

In the Soviet Union the nationalization of all aspects of private life has led to the destruction of the private and ultimately has created the public household. In the United States the privatization of most aspects of civil society has resulted in the disappearance of street and square as safe civic spaces and possibly of public space *tout court*. The desertion of the public realm is, in privileged areas, mitigated by an archipelago of privately owned and sponsored safe places in the form of shopping malls, hotel atria, office plazas, airport lounges, school campuses, culture and leisure places, and so on. These are to a neutral observer like safe-stations in a generally uncivil environment.

The bad news is that democracy is capable of colossal environmental blunders. The good news is that democracy is capable of learning through mistakes. The work of Duany and Plater-Zyberk is the first complete planning package to reorient national settlement and circulation policies. While their architectural products and images are incidental and adapted to local conditions, their legislative work is of national and constitutional relevance. It is not one option among many but so far the only alternative to the ecological and social wastage of routine development packages.

If the U.S. is to survive as more than a symbol of democracy, it will have to engage in a nationwide program of community building. This is not a choice but a necessity because the catastrophic growth of poverty and urban slums cannot be relieved by ever-expanding public welfare organizations and private charities; it must be relieved by the state looking after those who have no ability to fit the crude logic of corporate capitalism.

Growth and expansion are the imperatives of an industrial economy. The aggressive ambition of its leadership reflects this state of affairs and is its master. It has little understanding or time for that class of adults whose greatest ambition is to lead a modest life yet be their own boss. Those who don't fit into the regimented categories of leader and subordinate make up a substantial part of American society, and unless that society reforms into the inimitable disciplinarian model of Japan, there is no chance for this mass of passive dissidence to improve their human condition.

If the United States is to solve its social and environmental problems in the future, it must revise the whole national philosophy of settlement, the very notion of civil society. The small-town philosophy of the TND is not just an architectural paradigm, but a social synthesis which, if applied nationally, will allow a much larger range of people and talents to become active citizens, in the full meaning of that phrase. Only when this possibility is secured will the dreadful welfare bureaucracy wither away; only then can states and governments take up their original constitutional aim as guardian and patron of the *res publica* of the civic realm and its welfare.

Leon Krier is an architect, town planner, and urban theorist.

Many people have contributed to the preparation of this catalogue and exhibition. The efforts of the following individuals deserve special acknowledgement and thanks:

Monica Lynne O'Neal
Research Assistance

Margie Chin, Allen + Chin
Designer and Coordinator

Anne Mackin, Designwriting
Text Editor

Xavier Iglesias
Design and Production Assistance

Darell Fields
Curator of Lectures and Exhibitions

Kerry Herman
Coordinator of Lectures and Exhibitions

Susan McNally
Coordination Assistance

Illustrations in this catalogue have been provided by the owners or custodians of the work. The following have been provided with the courtesy of:

Peter Rowe, *Fig. 3, p. 9*
Frances Loeb Library, Harvard University
Graduate School of Design, *Fig. 5, p. 11; Figs. 12, 13, p. 13*
Anne Mackin, *Fig. 18, p. 15*
Lynn Pelham, *p. 110*
Philip Langdon, *p. 120*